Creative

Bible Study

Methods

HARVESTIME INTERNATIONAL INSTITUTE

This course is part of the **Harvestime International Institute**, a program designed to equip believers for effective spiritual harvest.

The basic theme of the training is to teach what Jesus taught, that which took men who were fishermen, tax collectors, etc., and changed them into reproductive Christians who reached their world with the Gospel in a demonstration of power.

This manual is a single course in one of several modules of curriculum which moves believers from visualizing through deputizing, multiplying, organizing, and mobilizing to achieve the goal of evangelizing.

For further information on additional courses write:

Harvestime International Institute
14431 Tierra Dr.
Colorado Springs, CO 80921
U.S.A.

TABLE OF CONTENTS

HOW TO USE THIS MANUAL

MANUAL FORMAT

Each lesson consists of:

Objectives: These are the goals you should achieve by studying the chapter. Read them before starting the lesson.

Key Verse: This verse emphasizes the main concept of the chapter. Memorize it.

Chapter Content: Study each section. Use your Bible to look up any references not printed in the manual.

Self-Test: Take this test after you finish studying the chapter. Try to answer the questions without using your Bible or this manual. When you have concluded the Self-Test, check your answers in the answer section provided at the end of the book.

For Further Study: This section will help you continue your study of the Word of God, improve your study skills, and apply what you have learned to your life and ministry.

Final Examination: If you are enrolled in this course for credit, you received a final examination along with this course. Upon conclusion of this course, you should complete this examination and return it for grading as instructed.

ADDITIONAL MATERIALS NEEDED

You will need a King James version of the Bible.

SUGGESTIONS FOR GROUP STUDY

FIRST MEETING

Opening: Open with prayer and introductions. Get acquainted and register the students.

Establish Group Procedures: Determine who will lead the meetings, the time, place, and dates for the sessions.

Praise And Worship: Invite the presence of the Holy Spirit into your training session.

Distribute Manuals To Students: Introduce the manual title, format, and course objectives provided in the first few pages of the manual.

Make The First Assignment: Students will read the chapters assigned and take the Self-Tests prior to the next meeting. The number of chapters you cover per meeting will depend on chapter length, content, and the abilities of your group.

SECOND AND FOLLOWING MEETINGS

Opening: Pray. Welcome and register any new students and give them a manual. Take attendance. Have a time of praise and worship.

Review: Present a brief summary of what you studied at the last meeting.

Lesson: Discuss each section of the chapter using the **HEADINGS IN CAPITAL BOLD FACED LETTERS** as a teaching outline. Ask students for questions or comments on what they have studied. Apply the lesson to the lives and ministries of your students.

Self-Test: Review the Self-Tests students have completed. (Note: If you do not want the students to have access to the answers to the Self-Tests, you may remove the answer pages from the back of each manual.)

For Further Study: You may do these projects on a group or individual basis.

Final Examination: If your group is enrolled in this course for credit, you received a final examination with this course. Reproduce a copy for each student and administer the exam upon conclusion of this course.

INTRODUCTION

The New Testament Prophet John the Baptist was known as a "voice crying in the wilderness" as he proclaimed the Word of God. His message was fresh, powerful, and relevant to the spiritual needs of his time.

Many people today have become echoes of spiritual truths they hear from those around them. They are not a voice through which God can reveal His message, but are only an echo of what they hear from others. They are like the prophets of whom God said, "steal my words every one from his neighbor" (Jeremiah 23:30).

In order to speak God's words you must first know what God has said. The purpose of this course is to equip you to understand God's Word. You will need only this manual, a Bible, and the guidance of the Holy Spirit to learn these "*Creative Bible Study Methods.*"

A method is an organized way to accomplish something. It is an orderly plan. Bible study methods are an organized plan to study God's written Word. The word "creative" means "having the ability to produce that which is new." This course teaches you how to study God's Word for yourself. You will not have to rely on the research of others because you will be able to create your own Bible studies based on your study of God's written Word.

By learning proper Bible study methods you will become a voice through which God can speak His truths to a spiritually hungry world. You will no longer only be an echo of what you hear from others.

"*Creative Bible Study Methods*" introduces the Bible as the written Word of the one true God. It explains divisions of the Bible, versions, translations, and paraphrases. First, the course guides you to discover what the Bible teaches about itself, then creative methods are explained and you are given the opportunity to use each method discussed.

The course also explains how to outline, make study notes, mark your Bible for easy reference, and reduce lengthy passages to simple charts. The course guides you to proper interpretation and application of God's Word. It directs attention to the greatest Teacher of all, the Holy Spirit. If you follow the guidelines presented, you will experience a new, creative spiritual life flowing within you.

No method of Bible study can replace the teaching ministry of the Holy Spirit. He is the spiritual force that endues a method with creative power. He whispers into the human spirit the truths of God's Word which create a new spiritual life flow.

The study of methods is not an end in itself. It is not the final goal. The methods are only a means to accomplish the objective of studying God's Word. It is not enough to learn these methods. You must use what you learn to study God's Word and apply its truths to your life and ministry.

Although you may complete the lessons in this manual, in reality you will never really complete this course. Your study of God's Word will never be finished because its rich spiritual truths can never be exhausted.

Note: This course teaches Bible study methods, not Bible content. Harvestime International Institute offers another course entitled "Basic Bible Survey" which presents the general background of the Bible, an outline of each book, its author, time of writing, to whom it was written, purpose, key verse, important characters, maps, dates, and charts summarizing general Bible content. Because of the need for a general introduction to the Bible in both Bible study and Bible survey, the first three chapters of these courses are identical while the remaining content differs.

COURSE OBJECTIVES

Upon completion of this course you will be able to:

- Explain how the Bible originated.

- Describe the organization of the Bible into testaments, major divisions, and books.

- Summarize basic history and chronology of the Bible.

- Explain the unity and diversity of the Bible.

- Explain how different Bible versions developed.

- Apply rules for proper interpretation of the Bible.

- Summarize what the Bible teaches about itself.

- Identify prerequisites for Bible study.

- Create outlines, charts, summaries, and text markings to help you retain content.

- Apply creative methods to your study of God's Word.

- Use Bible study tools.

CHAPTER ONE

INTRODUCING THE BIBLE

OBJECTIVES:

Upon completion of this chapter you will be able to:

- Write the Key Verse from memory.
- Define the word "Bible."
- Define the word "Scripture."
- Explain the origin of the Bible.
- Identify the major purposes of the Bible.
- Identify the Old and New Testaments as the two major divisions of the Bible.
- Name the four divisions of Old Testament books.
- Name the four divisions of New Testament books.
- Explain what is meant by the "unity and diversity" of the Bible.
- Identify the person upon whom the revelation of both testaments center.

KEY VERSES:

All Scripture is given by inspiration of God, and is profitable for doctrine, for reproof, for correction, for instruction in righteousness:

That the man of God may be perfect, thoroughly furnished unto all good works. (II Timothy 3:16-17)

INTRODUCTION

This chapter introduces the Bible which is the written Word of the one true God. The word "Bible" means "the books." The Bible is one volume which consists of 66 separate books.

The word "Scripture" is also used to refer to God's Word. This word comes from a Latin word which means "writing." When the word "Scripture" is used with a capital "S" it means the sacred writings of the one true God. The word "Bible" is not used in the Bible. It is a word used by men as a title for all of God's Words.

ORIGIN OF THE BIBLE

The Bible is the written Word of God. He inspired the words in the Bible and used approximately 40 different men to write down His words. These men wrote over a period of 1500 years. The perfect agreement of these writers is one proof that they were all guided by a single author. That author was God.

Some of the writers wrote down exactly what God said:

> **Take thee a roll of a book, and write therein all the words that I have spoken unto thee against Israel . . . (Jeremiah 36:2)**

Other writers wrote what they experienced or what God revealed concerning the future:

> **Write the things which thou hast seen, and the things which are, and the things which shall be hereafter. (Revelation 1:19)**

All of the writers wrote under God's inspiration the words of His message for us.

THE PURPOSE OF THE BIBLE

The Bible itself records its main purpose:

> **All Scripture is given by inspiration of God, and is profitable for doctrine, for reproof, for correction, for instruction in righteousness:**
>
> **That the man of God may be perfect, thoroughly furnished unto all good works. (II Timothy 3:16-17)**

The Scriptures are to be used to teach doctrine, to reprove and correct from evil, and to teach righteousness. They will help you live right and equip you to work for God.

MAJOR DIVISIONS

The Bible is divided into two major sections called the Old Testament and the New Testament. The word "testament" means "covenant." A covenant is an agreement. The Old Testament records God's original covenant or agreement with man. The New Testament records the new covenant made by God through His Son, Jesus Christ.

What was the subject of these two agreements? They both concerned restoring sinful man to right relationship with God. God made a law that sin can only be forgiven through the shedding of blood:

. . . without shedding of blood is no remission (forgiveness). (Hebrews 9:22)

Under God's agreement in the Old Testament, blood sacrifices of animals were made by man to obtain forgiveness for sin. This was a symbol of the blood sacrifice Jesus Christ would provide under the new agreement with God. Through the birth, life, death, and resurrection of Jesus, a final sacrifice for sin was made:

> **But Christ being come an high priest of good things to come, by a greater and more perfect tabernacle, not made with hands, that is to say, not of this building;**
>
> **Neither by the blood of goats and calves, but by His own blood He entered in once into the holy place, having obtained eternal redemption for us.**
>
> **For if the blood of bulls and of goats, and the ashes of an heifer sprinkling the unclean, sanctifieth to the purifying of the flesh:**
>
> **How much more shall the blood of Christ, who through the eternal Spirit offered Himself without spot to God, purge your conscience from dead works to serve the living God?**
>
> **And for this cause He is the mediator of the new testament, that by means of death, for the redemption the transgressions that were under the first testament, they which are called might receive the promise of eternal inheritance. (Hebrews 9:11-15)**

Both testaments are the Word of God and we must study both in order to understand God's message. The terms "old" and "new" testaments are used to distinguish between God's agreement with man before and after the death of Jesus Christ. We do not disregard the Old Testament simply because it is called "old."

FURTHER DIVISIONS

The Bible is further divided into 66 books. The Old Testament has 39 books. The New Testament contains 27 books. Each book is divided into chapters and verses. Although the content of each book is the Word of God, the division into chapters and verses was made by man to make it easy to locate specific passages. It would be very difficult to find a passage if the books were all one long paragraph.

Here is a simple diagram that shows the basic divisions of the Bible:

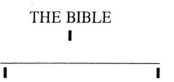

THE BIBLE

Old Testament   New Testament
39 Books   27 Books

UNITY OF THE BIBLE

When we speak of the unity of the Bible, we mean two things:

ONE: THE BIBLE IS UNITED IN CONTENT:

Even though the Bible was written by many writers over many years, there are no contradictions. One author does not contradict any of the others.

The Bible includes discussion of hundreds of controversial subjects. (A controversial subject is one that creates different opinions when mentioned). Yet the writers of the Bible spoke on such subjects with harmony from the first book of Genesis through the last book of Revelation. This was possible because there was really only one author: God. The writers only recorded the message under His direction and inspiration. For this reason, the content of the Bible is united.

TWO: THE BIBLE IS UNITED IN THEME:

Some people think the Bible is a collection of 66 separate books on different subjects. They do not realize that the Bible is united by a major theme. From beginning to end, the Bible reveals God's special purpose which is summarized in the book of Ephesians:

> **Having made known unto us the mystery of His will, according to His good pleasure which He hath purposed in Himself:**
>
> **That in the dispensation of the fullness of times He might gather together in one all things in Christ, both which are in heaven, and which are on earth; even in Him:**
>
> **In whom also we have obtained an inheritance, being predestinated according to the purpose of Him who worketh all things after the counsel of His own will. (Ephesians 1:9-11)**

The Bible reveals the mystery of God's plan which is the unifying theme of the Bible. It is the revelation of Jesus Christ as the Savior of sinful mankind. Jesus explained how the Old Testament centered on Him:

And He said unto them, These are the words which I spake unto you while I was yet with you, that all things must be fulfilled, which were written in the law of Moses, and in the prophets, and in the psalms concerning me. (Luke 24:44)

With this introduction, Jesus continued and . . .

. . . opened He their understanding that they might understand the scriptures. (Luke 24:45)

What was the key Jesus gave them to understanding the Scriptures? The fact that its major theme focused on Him:

. . . Thus it is written, and thus it behooved Christ to suffer, and to rise from the dead the third day:

And that repentance and remission of sins should be preached in His name among all nations, beginning at Jerusalem. And Ye are witnesses of these things. (Luke 24:46-4)

The Old and New Testaments both tell the story of Jesus. The Old Testament prepares us for its happening and the New Testament tells how it happened. This unites the Bible in one major theme. The people who looked forward to Jesus under the Old Testament were saved from their sins through faith in God's promise. Everyone who looks back to it as having been fulfilled in Jesus Christ is saved in the same way: Through faith that it happened just as God promised.

DIVERSITY OF THE BIBLE

When we speak of the "diversity" of the Bible we mean that the Bible has variety. It records different ways in which God dealt with people and the different ways in which they responded to Him.

The Bible is written in different moods. Some portions express joy while others reflect sorrow. The Bible includes different types of writing. It contains history, poetry, prophecy, letters, adventure, parables, miracles, and love stories. Because of its variety, the Bible has been further divided into major groups of books.

OLD TESTAMENT DIVISIONS

The books of the Old Testament are divided into four major groups: Law, history, poetry and prophecy.

THE BOOKS OF THE LAW:

There are five books of law. The names of these books are:

> Genesis
> Exodus
> Leviticus
> Numbers
> Deuteronomy

These books record the creation of man and the world by God and the early history of man. They tell how God raised up the nation of Israel as a people through which He could reveal Himself to the nations of the world.

These books record the laws of God. The best known parts are the Ten Commandments (Exodus 20:3-17), the greatest of all commandments (Deuteronomy 6:5), and the second greatest commandment (Leviticus 19:18).

Open your Bible and locate the books of Law in the Old Testament. Locate the three verses mentioned in the preceding paragraph and read them. These are an example of the laws of God recorded in these books.

THE BOOKS OF HISTORY:

There are 12 books of history in the Old Testament. The names of the books of history are:

> Joshua
> Judges
> Ruth
> I and II Samuel
> I and II Kings
> I and II Chronicles
> Ezra
> Nehemiah
> Esther

Locate these books in your Bible. They are found right after the books of law. The books of history cover a thousand year history of God's people, Israel. Naturally they do not tell everything that happened, but they record the major events and show the results of both following and ignoring God's law.

THE BOOKS OF POETRY:

There are five books of poetry. The names of the books of poetry are:

Job
Psalms
Proverbs
Ecclesiastes
Song of Solomon

These books are the worship books of God's people, Israel. They still are used in worship by believers today. Turn to Psalm 23 and read it. This is an example of the beautiful worship poetry contained in these books.

THE BOOKS OF PROPHECY:

The books of prophecy of the Old Testament are divided into two groups which are called Major and Minor prophetical books. This does not mean the Major Prophets are more important than the Minor Prophets. The title is simply used because the Major Prophets are longer books than the Minor Prophets. There are 17 books of prophecy in the Old Testament. The names of the books of prophecy are:

Major Prophets:

Isaiah
Jeremiah
Lamentations
Ezekiel
Daniel

Minor Prophets:

Hosea	Nahum
Joel	Habakkuk
Amos	Zechariah
Obadiah	Haggai
Jonah	Zechariah
Micah	Malachi

These books are prophetic messages from God to His people about future events. Many of the prophecies have already been fulfilled, but some remain to be fulfilled in the future. Find these prophetic books in your Bible. They are the last books in the Old Testament.

NEW TESTAMENT DIVISIONS

The New Testament has also been divided into four groups: Gospels, History, Letters, and Prophecy.

THE GOSPELS:

There are four books in the Gospels. The names of these books are:

Matthew   Mark   Luke   John

These books tell about the life, death, and resurrection of Jesus. Their purpose is to lead you to believe that He is the Christ, the Son of God. Find the Gospels in your Bible and then read John 20:31 which states this purpose.

THE BOOK OF HISTORY:

There is one book of history in the New Testament, the book of Acts. This book tells how the church began and fulfilled Christ's commission to spread the Gospel throughout the world. Locate this book in your Bible.

LETTERS:

There are 21 letters in the New Testament. The names of these letters are:

Romans	Titus
I and II Corinthians	Philemon
Galatians	Hebrews
Ephesians	James
Philippians	I and II Peter
Colossians	I, II, and III John
I and II Thessalonians	Jude
I and II Timothy	

The letters are addressed to all believers. Their purpose is to guide them in living and help them do what Jesus commanded. Romans 12 is a good example of their teaching. Turn to this chapter in your Bible and read it. The letters are also sometimes called "epistles" which means letters.

PROPHECY:

Revelation is the only book of prophecy in the New Testament. It tells of the final victory of Jesus and His people. Its purpose is to encourage you to keep living as a Christian should live until the end of time. Its message is summarized in Revelation 2:10.

SELF-TEST

1. Write the Key Verses from memory:

_____

_____

_____

_____

2. What does the word "Bible" mean?_____

3. What does the word "Scripture" mean?_____

4. What are the two major divisions of the Bible?

_____   _____

5. How many books are there in the Bible?_____

6. Name the four major groups into which Old Testament books are divided:

_____   _____

_____   _____

7. Name the four major groups into which New Testament books are divided:

_____   _____

_____   _____

8. What is the meaning of the word "testament"?

_____

_____

9. What are four main purposes of the Bible? Give a Bible reference to support your answer.

_____

_____

_____

_____

10. What is meant by the "unity of the Bible"?

_____

11. What is meant by the "diversity of the Bible"?

_____

12. Read each statement. If the statement is TRUE put the letter T on the blank in front of it. If the statement is FALSE put the letter F on the blank in front of it:

a._____The Bible is the written Word of the one true God.

b._____Although God inspired the Bible, He used men to write down His words.

c._____Because there were many writers over a period of many years, the Bible contains a lot of contradictions.

d._____There is no united theme of the Bible. It is just a collection of books on different subjects.

e._____The Major Prophets of the Old Testament are more important than the Minor Prophets.

13. Who is the person on which the revelation of both testaments centers? Give a Bible

reference to support your answer._____Reference_____

(Answers to tests are provided at the conclusion of the final chapter in this manual.)

FOR FURTHER STUDY

The bookmarks on the next page will help you learn the major divisions of the Bible. Cut out the bookmarks on the lines dividing them and place them in your Bible. If you have difficulty in locating the place to insert your bookmarks, use the Table of Contents in the front of your Bible. It lists the books in the order in which they appear in the Bible. It also provides the page number where each book begins.

OLD TESTAMENT

Place bookmark 1 at the beginning of the book of Genesis.

Place bookmark 2 at the beginning of the book of Joshua.

Place bookmark 3 at the beginning of the book of Job.

Place bookmark 4 at the beginning of the book of Isaiah.

NEW TESTAMENT

Place bookmark 5 at the beginning of the book of Matthew.

Place bookmark 6 at the beginning of the book of Acts.

Place bookmark 7 at the beginning of the book of Romans.

Place bookmark 8 at the beginning of the book of Revelation.

You have now located the major divisions of the Bible. Keep using the bookmarks until you can name and locate these divisions by memory.

OLD TESTAMENT LAW (1)	OLD TESTAMENT HISTORY (2)	OLD TESTAMENT POETRY (3)
GENESIS EXODUS LEVITICUS NUMBERS DEUTERONOMY	JOSHUA JUDGES RUTH I SAMUEL II SAMUEL I KINGS II KINGS I CHRONICLES II CHRONICLES EZRA NEHEMIAH ESTHER	JOB PSALMS PROVERBS ECCLESIASTES SONG OF SOLOMON

OLD TESTAMENT PROPHECY (4)

<u>MAJOR PROPHETS</u>:
ISAIAH
JEREMIAH
LAMENTATIONS
EZEKIEL
DANIEL

<u>MINOR PROPHETS</u>:
HOSEA
JOEL
AMOS
OBADIAH
JONAH
MICAH
NAHUM
HABAKKUK
ZECHARIAH
HAGGAI
ZECHARIAH
MALACHI

<u>OLD TESTAMENT BOOK MARKS</u>

NEW TESTAMENT GOSPELS (5)	NEW TESTAMENT HISTORY (6)	NEW TESTAMENT LETTERS (7)
MATTHEW MARK LUKE JOHN	ACTS	ROMANS I CORINTHIANS II CORINTHIANS GALATIANS EPHESIANS PHILIPPIANS COLOSSIANS I THESSALONIANS II THESSALONIANS I TIMOTHY II TIMOTHY TITUS PHILEMON HEBREWS JAMES I PETER II PETER I JOHN II JOHN III JOHN JUDE

NEW TESTAMENT PROPHECY (8)

REVELATION

NEW TESTAMENT BOOK MARKS

16

CHAPTER TWO

THE BOOKS OF THE BIBLE

OBJECTIVES:

Upon completion of this chapter you will be able to:

- Write the Key Verse from memory.
- Identify the number of books in the Old Testament.
- Identify the number of books in the New Testament.
- Explain why it is important to have a systematic plan for reading the Bible.
- List four suggestions for successful Bible reading.

KEY VERSE:

Let my cry come near before thee, O Lord: give me understanding according to thy Word. (Psalm 119:169)

INTRODUCTION

In the previous chapter you learned that the Bible is the written Word of God. You learned it is divided into two major sections called the Old Testament and the New Testament. You learned the four divisions of the Old Testament books:

Law
History
Poetry
Prophecy

You also learned the four divisions of the New Testament books:

Gospels
History
Letters
Prophecy

The following chart summarizes what you have learned about the Bible so far:

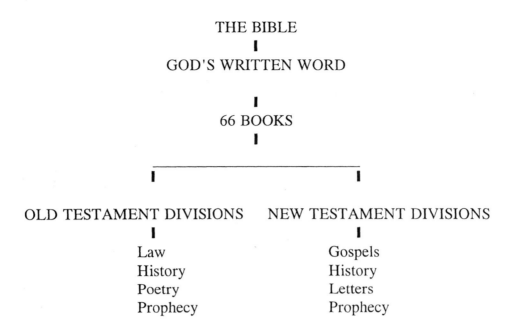

THE BIBLE
|
GOD'S WRITTEN WORD

|
66 BOOKS
|

OLD TESTAMENT DIVISIONS   NEW TESTAMENT DIVISIONS
| |
Law   Gospels
History   History
Poetry   Letters
Prophecy   Prophecy

This chapter contains a summary of each of the 66 books of the Bible which make up the major divisions of the Old and New Testaments. It provides an introduction to the content of both testaments. Four suggestions for successful Bible reading are given and you will choose a systematic plan to start reading God's Word.

OLD TESTAMENT BOOKS
(39 Books)

BOOKS OF LAW:

Genesis: Records the beginning of the universe, man, the Sabbath, marriage, sin, sacrifice, nations, and government and key men of God like Abraham, Isaac, Jacob, and Joseph.

Exodus: Details how Israel became a nation with Moses as leader. Israel is delivered from bondage in Egypt and travels to Mt. Sinai where the law of God is given.

Leviticus: This book was a manual of worship for Israel. It provides instruction to the religious leaders and explains how a sinful people can approach a righteous God. It relates to the coming of Jesus Christ as the Lamb of God who takes away the sins of the world.

Numbers: Records Israel's 40 years of wandering in the wilderness which was a result of disobedience to God. The title of the book is from two numberings (population censuses) taken during the long journey.

Deuteronomy: Records the final days of Moses' life and reviews the laws given in Exodus and Leviticus.

BOOKS OF HISTORY:

Joshua: Details how Joshua, the successor of Moses, led the people of Israel into the Promised Land of Canaan. It records the military campaigns and the division of the land among the people.

Judges: Israel turned away from God after Joshua's death. This book records the sad story of their repeated sins and the judges God raised up to deliver them from enemy forces.

Ruth: The story of Ruth, a woman of the Gentile nation of Moab, who chose to serve the God of Israel. She became the great grandmother of David.

I Samuel: This book centers on three persons: Samuel who was the last of the judges of Israel; Saul, the first king of Israel; and David who succeeded Saul as king.

II Samuel: The glorious 40 year reign of King David is recorded in this book.

I Kings: King Solomon's reign and the kings of the divided kingdom through the reigns of Ahab in the north and Jehoshaphat in the south are the subjects of this book.

II Kings: The final decline of Israel and Judah is recalled in this book. God's people fell into deep sin.

I Chronicles: The reign of David and preparations for building the temple are recorded here. The time of this book is the same as II Samuel.

II Chronicles: This book continues Israel's history through Solomon's reign with focus on the southern kingdom. It closes with the decree of Cyrus which permitted the return of the people from Babylon to Jerusalem.

Ezra: The return of the Jews from Babylonian captivity is detailed.

Nehemiah: The rebuilding of Jerusalem's walls under the direction of Nehemiah is recalled by this book. The project was begun about 14 years after Ezra's return with the people.

Esther: God's deliverance of the Jews through Esther and Mordecai is the subject of this book.

BOOKS OF POETRY:

Job: This book is the story of Job, a man who lived around the time of Abraham. The theme is the question of why righteous men suffer.

Psalms: The prayer and praise book of the Bible.

Proverbs: Divine wisdom for practical problems of everyday life.

Ecclesiastes: A discussion of the futility of life apart from God.

Song Of Solomon: The romance of Solomon and his Shulamite bride. The story represents God's love for Israel and of Christ for the church.

BOOKS OF PROPHECY:

Several of these books were written during a period when the nation of Israel was divided into two separate kingdoms: Israel and Judah.

Isaiah: Warns of coming judgment against Judah because of their sin against God.

Jeremiah: Written during the later decline and fall of Judah. Told of the coming judgment and urged surrender to Nebuchadnezzar.

Lamentations: Jeremiah's lament (expression of sorrow) over the destruction of Jerusalem by Babylon.

Ezekiel: Warns first of Jerusalem's impending fall and then foretells its future restoration.

Daniel: The prophet Daniel was captured during the early siege of Judah and taken to Babylon. This book provides historic and prophetic teaching which is important in understanding Bible prophecy.

Hosea: Theme of this book is Israel's unfaithfulness, their punishment, and restoration by God.

Joel: Tells of the plagues which foreshadowed future judgment.

Amos: During a period of material prosperity but moral decay, Amos warned Israel and surrounding nations of God's future judgment on their sin.

Obadiah: God's judgment against Edom, an evil nation located south of the Dead Sea.

Jonah: The story of the prophet Jonah who preached repentance in Ninevah, capitol of the Assyrian empire. The book reveals God's love and plan of repentance for the Gentiles.

Micah: Another prophecy against Israel's sin. Foretells the birthplace of Jesus 700 years before the event happened.

Nahum: Tells of the impending destruction of Ninevah which had been spared some 150 years earlier through Jonah's preaching.

Habakkuk: Reveals God's plan to punish a sinful nation by an even more sinful one. Teaches that "the just shall live by faith."

Zephaniah: Judgment and restoration of Judah.

Haggai: Urges the Jews to rebuild the temple after a 15 year delay due to enemy resistance.

Zechariah: Further urging to complete the temple and renew spiritual commitment. Foretells Christ's first and second comings.

Malachi: Warns against spiritual shallowness and foretells the coming of John the Baptist and Jesus.

NEW TESTAMENT BOOKS
(27 Books)

THE GOSPELS:

The four books known as the Gospels record the birth, life, ministry, teachings, death and resurrection of Jesus Christ. The approach of each book differs:

Matthew: Emphasizes Jesus Christ as King and was directed especially to the Jews.

Mark: Emphasizes Jesus Christ as the Servant of God and was directed especially to the Romans.

Luke: Presents Jesus Christ as the "Son of Man," the perfect man and Savior of imperfect men.

John: Presents Jesus in His position as the Son of God.

BOOK OF HISTORY:

Acts: The one history book of the New Testament records the early growth of Christianity from the time of Christ's return to Heaven through Paul's imprisonment in Rome. The book covers about 33 years and emphasizes the work of the Holy Spirit.

LETTERS:

Romans: A presentation of the Gospel which stresses salvation by faith alone.

I Corinthians: Written to correct errors of Christian conduct in the local church.

II Corinthians: Speaks of the true ministry of the Gospel, stewardship, and Paul's apostolic authority.

Galatians: Deals with the error of mixing law and faith. The theme is justification by faith alone.

Ephesians: Encourages believers regarding their position in Christ.

Philippians: Emphasizes the joy of the Christian unity.

Colossians: Deals with the error of "Gnosticism," a false teachings which denied Jesus was truly Son of God and Son of Man. The book also emphasizes Jesus as head of the Church.

I Thessalonians: Counsel in Christian living and emphasis on the return of Jesus.

II Thessalonians: Further instruction on the Lord's return and how knowledge of this should affect everyday life.

I Timothy: Stresses sound doctrine, orderly church government, and principles to guide the church in the years to come.

II Timothy: Describes the true servant of Jesus Christ. It also warns of the apostasy (spiritual decline) which had already started. It presents the Word of God as the remedy to correct all error.

Titus: Paul's letter to a young minister named Titus who was serving God on the island of Crete. Doctrine and a Godly life are stressed.

Philemon: Paul's intercession for a runaway slave of a wealthy Colossian Christian. It illustrates the intercession of Jesus on the behalf of believers who were once slaves to sin.

Hebrews: Explains the superiority of Christianity over Judaism. Presents Jesus as the Great High Priest and the mediator between God and man.

James: Teaches that true faith is evidenced by works, although salvation is by faith alone.

I Peter: A letter of comfort and encouragement to believers, especially those suffering spiritual attacks from outside the church through unbelievers.

II Peter: A warning against spiritual attacks from within. For example, false teachers who had already "crept" into the Church.

I John: Written to combat Gnosticism which denied Christ's position as Son of God and Son of Man. The book emphasizes fellowship and love among believers and assures true believers of eternal life.

II John: Warns against any compromise with doctrinal error and emphasizes that the truth must be guarded in love.

III John: Warns of the sin of refusing fellowship with those who are true believers.

Jude: Another warning against apostasy and false doctrine. The theme is similar to that of II Peter.

BOOK OF PROPHECY:

Revelation: This prophetic book tells of the final events of world history. It tells of the things which were, are, and which will be in the future plan of God (Revelation 4:22).

SUCCESSFUL BIBLE READING

You will learn much in this course about how to understand and interpret the Bible. You will also learn methods of creative Bible study. But the first step in understanding the Bible is to begin to read it. To help you start reading God's Word we have outlined several different reading plans. These include a plan for those just starting their study as well as a plan for those who are more advanced in the study of God's Word. First, here are four suggestions for successful Bible reading:

1. READ DAILY:

> **But his delight is in the law of the Lord; and in His law doth he meditate day and night. (Psalm 1:2)**

God made your physical body so you must have food daily in order to remain healthy. In a similar manner, your spirit must be fed daily with the food of the Word of God if you are to be spiritually healthy:

> **. . . It is written, That man shall not live by bread alone, but by every Word of God. (Luke 4:4)**

2. READ SELECTIVELY:

Start by reading the "milk" of the word. These are the simple truths of the Word of God:

> **As newborn babes, desire the sincere milk of the Word that ye may grow thereby. (I Peter 2:2)**

Later you will mature spiritually to where you can eat "meat" of the Word of God. This means you will be able to understand more difficult teachings of the Bible:

For everyone that useth milk is unskillful in the word of righteousness: for he is a babe.

But strong meat belongeth to them that are of full age, even those who by reason of use have their senses exercised to discern both good and evil. (Hebrews 5:13-14)

I have fed you with milk, and not with meat: for hitherto ye were not able to bear it . . . (I Corinthians 3:2)

3. READ PRAYERFULLY:

For Ezra had prepared his heart to seek the law of the Lord. (Ezra 7:10)

Before you start to read, pray to God and ask Him to help you understand the message He has given you through His written Word. Let your prayer be as the Psalmist David prayed:

Open thou mine eyes, that I may behold wondrous things out of thy law. (Psalm 119:18)

4. READ SYSTEMATICALLY:

Some people do not understand God's Word because they do not have a systematic plan for reading. They read a chapter here and there and fail to understand how it all fits together. This is like reading a few pages here and there in a text book on medicine and then trying to set up a medical practice. The Bible tells us to "search the scriptures" (John 5:39). This means to study them carefully. The Bible is like a text book used in school. You must read it in an orderly way if you are to understand its content. Select one of the following reading schedules and begin reading your Bible daily.

FOR BEGINNERS

If you have never read the Bible before, start with the book of John in the New Testament. This book was written by one of the Disciples of Jesus Christ named John. He tells the story of Jesus in a simple way which is easy to understand.

Read one chapter in John each day in the order in which they are found in your Bible. Use the following chart to check off each chapter as you read it.

The Gospel Of John:

_____1	_____5	_____9	_____13	_____17
_____2	_____6	_____10	_____14	_____18
_____3	_____7	_____11	_____15	_____19
_____4	_____8	_____12	_____16	_____20

THE SHORT SCHEDULE

The short schedule of Bible reading is designed to provide a basic knowledge of the Bible through selected portions of Scripture. Read the selected portions in the order in which they are listed. Use the chart to check off each portion as you complete your reading.

THE NEW TESTAMENT:

_____John   _____I Thessalonians   _____Ephesians

_____Mark   _____I Corinthians   _____II Timothy

_____Luke   _____Romans   _____I Peter

_____Acts   _____Philemon   _____I John

_____Romans   _____Philippians   _____Revelation 1-5; 19:6-22:21

THE OLD TESTAMENT:

_____Genesis   _____Amos

_____Exodus 1-20   _____Isaiah 1-12

_____Numbers 10:11-21:35   _____Jeremiah 1-25;39-33

_____Deuteronomy 1-11   _____Ruth

_____Joshua 1-12; 22-24   _____Jonah

_____Judges 1-3   _____Psalms 1-23

_____I Samuel 1-3, 9-10,1 3,15-18,31   _____Job 1-14, 38-42

_____II Samuel 1   _____Proverbs 1-9

_____I Kings 1-11   _____Daniel 1-6

_____Nehemiah

THE LONGER SCHEDULE

This reading plan covers the Bible in greater depth than the Short Schedule, but it does not cover the entire Bible.

NEW TESTAMENT:

_____Mark	_____Philippians
_____Matthew	_____Ephesians
_____John	_____II Timothy
_____Luke	_____Titus
_____Acts	_____I Timothy
_____I Thessalonians	_____I Peter
_____II Thessalonians	_____Hebrews
_____I Corinthians	_____James
_____II Corinthians	_____I John
_____Galatians	_____II John
_____Romans	_____III John
_____Philemon	_____Jude
_____Colossians	_____II Peter
	_____Revelation 1-5 and 19:6-22:21

(The Longer Schedule Continued)
OLD TESTAMENT:

_____Genesis

_____Exodus 1-24

_____Leviticus 1-6:7

_____Numbers 10:11-21:35

_____Deuteronomy 1-11 and 27-34

_____Joshua 1-12 and 22-24

_____Judges 1-16

_____I Samuel

_____II Samuel

_____I Kings

_____II Kings

_____I Chronicles

_____II Chronicles

_____Ezra

_____Nehemiah

_____Amos

_____Hosea

_____Micah

_____Isaiah 1-12

_____Zephaniah

_____Jeremiah 1-25 and 30-33

_____Nahum

_____Habakkuk

_____Ezekiel 1-24 and 33-39

_____Obadiah

_____Lamentations

_____Isaiah 40-66

_____Zechariah 1-8

_____Malachi

_____Joel

_____Ruth

_____Jonah

_____Psalms

_____Job

_____Proverbs 1-9

_____Song of Solomon

_____Ecclesiastes

_____Esther

_____Daniel

THE COMPLETE SCHEDULE

The complete Bible reading schedule takes you through the entire Bible in one year.

January

_____	1.	Genesis 1-2
_____	2.	Genesis 3-5
_____	3.	Genesis 6-9
_____	4.	Genesis 10-11
_____	5.	Genesis 12-15
_____	6.	Genesis 16-19
_____	7.	Genesis 20-22
_____	8.	Genesis 23-26
_____	9.	Genesis 27-29
_____	10.	Genesis 30-32
_____	11.	Genesis 33-36
_____	12.	Genesis 37-39
_____	13.	Genesis 40-42
_____	14.	Genesis 43-46
_____	15.	Genesis 47-50
_____	16.	Job 1-4
_____	17.	Job 5-7
_____	18.	Job 8-10
_____	19.	Job ll-13
_____	20.	Job 14-17
_____	21.	Job 18-20
_____	22.	Job 21-24
_____	23.	Job 25-27
_____	24.	Job 28-31
_____	25.	Job 32-34
_____	26.	Job 35-37
_____	27.	Job 38-42
_____	28.	Exodus 1-4
_____	29.	Exodus 5-7
_____	30.	Exodus 8-10
_____	31.	Exodus 11-13

February

_____	1.	Exodus 14-17
_____	2.	Exodus 18-20
_____	3.	Exodus 21-24
_____	4.	Exodus 25-27
_____	5.	Exodus 28-31
_____	6.	Exodus 32-34
_____	7.	Exodus 35-37
_____	8.	Exodus 38-40
_____	9.	Leviticus 1-4
_____	10.	Leviticus 5-7
_____	11.	Leviticus 8-10
_____	12.	Leviticus 11-13
_____	13.	Leviticus 14-16
_____	14.	Leviticus 17-19
_____	15.	Leviticus 20-23
_____	16.	Leviticus 24-27
_____	17.	Numbers 1-3
_____	18.	Numbers 4-6
_____	19.	Numbers 7-10
_____	20.	Numbers 11-14
_____	21.	Numbers 15-17
_____	22.	Numbers 18-20
_____	23.	Numbers 21-24
_____	24.	Numbers 25-27
_____	25.	Numbers 28-30
_____	26.	Numbers 31-33
_____	27.	Numbers 34-36
_____	28.	Deuteronomy 1-3

(The Complete Schedule Continued)

March		**April**	
_____ 1.	Deuteronomy 4-6	_____ 1.	I Samuel 21-24
_____ 2.	Deuteronomy 7-9	_____ 2.	I Samuel 25-28
_____ 3.	Deuteronomy 10-12	_____ 3.	I Samuel 29-31
_____ 4.	Deuteronomy 13-16	_____ 4.	II Samuel 1-4
_____ 5.	Deuteronomy 17-19	_____ 5.	II Samuel 5-8
_____ 6.	Deuteronomy 20-22	_____ 6.	II Samuel 9-12
_____ 7.	Deuteronomy 23-25	_____ 7.	II Samuel 13-15
_____ 8.	Deuteronomy 26-28	_____ 8.	II Samuel 16-18
_____ 9.	Deuteronomy 29-31	_____ 9.	II Samuel 19-21
_____ 10.	Deuteronomy 32-34	_____ 10.	II Samuel 22-24
_____ 11.	Joshua 1-3	_____ 11.	Psalms 1-3
_____ 12.	Joshua 4-6	_____ 12.	Psalms 4-6
_____ 13.	Joshua 7-9	_____ 13.	Psalms 7-9
_____ 14.	Joshua 10-12	_____ 14.	Psalms 10-12
_____ 15.	Joshua 13-15	_____ 15.	Psalms 13-15
_____ 16.	Joshua 16-18	_____ 16.	Psalms 16-18
_____ 17.	Joshua 19-21	_____ 17.	Psalms 19-21
_____ 18.	Joshua 22-24	_____ 18.	Psalms 22-24
_____ 19.	Judges 1-4	_____ 19.	Psalms 25-27
_____ 20.	Judges 5-8	_____ 20.	Psalms 28-30
_____ 21.	Judges 9-12	_____ 21.	Psalms 31-33
_____ 22.	Judges 13-15	_____ 22.	Psalms 34-36
_____ 23.	Judges 16-18	_____ 23.	Psalms 37-39
_____ 24.	Judges 19-21	_____ 24.	Psalms 40-42
_____ 25.	Ruth 1-4	_____ 25.	Psalms 43-45
_____ 26.	I Samuel 1-3	_____ 26.	Psalms 46-48
_____ 27.	I Samuel 4-7	_____ 27.	Psalms 49-51
_____ 28.	I Samuel 8-10	_____ 28.	Psalms 52-54
_____ 29.	I Samuel 11-13	_____ 29.	Psalms 55-57
_____ 30.	I Samuel 14-16	_____ 30.	Psalms 58-60
_____ 31.	I Samuel 17-20		

(The Complete Schedule Continued)

	May		**June**
_____ 1.	Psalms 61-63	_____ 1.	Proverbs 1-3
_____ 2.	Psalms 64-66	_____ 2.	Proverbs 4-7
_____ 3.	Psalms 67-69	_____ 3.	Proverbs 8-11
_____ 4.	Psalms 70-72	_____ 4.	Proverbs 12-14
_____ 5.	Psalms 73-75	_____ 5.	Proverbs 15-18
_____ 6.	Psalms 76-78	_____ 6.	Proverbs 19-21
_____ 7.	Psalms 79-81	_____ 7.	Proverbs 22-24
_____ 8.	Psalms 82-84	_____ 8.	Proverbs 25-28
_____ 9.	Psalms 85-87	_____ 9.	Proverbs 29-31
_____ 10.	Psalms 88-90	_____ 10.	Ecclesiastes 1-3
_____ 11.	Psalms 91-93	_____ 11.	Ecclesiastes 4-6
_____ 12.	Psalms 94-96	_____ 12.	Ecclesiastes 7-9
_____ 13.	Psalms 97-99	_____ 13.	Ecclesiastes 10-12
_____ 14.	Psalms 100-102	_____ 14.	Songs 1-4
_____ 15.	Psalms 103-105	_____ 15.	Songs 5-8
_____ 16.	Psalms 106-108	_____ 16.	I Kings 5-7
_____ 17.	Psalms 109-111	_____ 17.	I Kings 8-10
_____ 18.	Psalms 112-114	_____ 18.	I Kings 11-13
_____ 19.	Psalms 115-118	_____ 19.	I Kings 14-16
_____ 20.	Psalm 119	_____ 20.	I Kings 17-19
_____ 21.	Psalms 120-123	_____ 21.	I Kings 20-22
_____ 22.	Psalms 124-126	_____ 22.	II Kings 1-3
_____ 23.	Psalms 127-129	_____ 23.	II Kings 4-6
_____ 24.	Psalms 130-132	_____ 24.	II Kings 7-10
_____ 25.	Psalms 133-135	_____ 25.	II Kings 11-14:20
_____ 26.	Psalms 136-138	_____ 26.	Joel 1-3
_____ 27.	Psalms 139-141	_____ 27.	II Kings 14:21-25; Jonah 1-4
_____ 28.	Psalms 142-144	_____ 28.	II Kings 14:26-29; Amos 1-3
_____ 29.	Psalms 145-147	_____ 29.	Amos 4-6
_____ 30.	Psalms 148-150	_____ 30.	Amos 7-9
_____ 31.	I Kings 1-4		

(The Complete Schedule Continued)

	July			**August**	
___	1.	II Kings 15-17	___	1.	II Kings 20-21
___	2.	Hosea 1-4	___	2.	Zephaniah 1-3
___	3.	Hosea 5-7	___	3.	Habakkuk 1-3
___	4.	Hosea 8-10	___	4.	II Kings 22-25
___	5.	Hosea 11-14	___	5.	Obadiah/Jeremiah 1-2
___	6.	II Kings 18-19	___	6.	Jeremiah 3-5
___	7.	Isaiah 1-3	___	7.	Jeremiah 6-8
___	8.	Isaiah 4-6	___	8.	Jeremiah 9-12
___	9.	Isaiah 7-9	___	9.	Jeremiah 13-16
___	10.	Isaiah 10-12	___	10.	Jeremiah 17-20
___	11.	Isaiah 13-15	___	11.	Jeremiah 21-23
___	12.	Isaiah 16-18	___	12.	Jeremiah 24-26
___	13.	Isaiah 19-21	___	13.	Jeremiah 27-29
___	14.	Isaiah 22-24	___	14.	Jeremiah 30-32
___	15.	Isaiah 25-27	___	15.	Jeremiah 33-36
___	16.	Isaiah 28-30	___	16.	Jeremiah 37-39
___	17.	Isaiah 31-33	___	17.	Jeremiah 40-42
___	18.	Isaiah 34-36	___	18.	Jeremiah 43-46
___	19.	Isaiah 37-39	___	19.	Jeremiah 47-49
___	20.	Isaiah 40-42	___	20.	Jeremiah 50-52
___	21.	Isaiah 43-45	___	21.	Lamentations 1-5
___	22.	Isaiah 46-48	___	22.	I Chronicles 1-3
___	23.	Isaiah 49-51	___	23.	I Chronicles 4-6
___	24.	Isaiah 52-54	___	24.	I Chronicles 7-9
___	25.	Isaiah 55-57	___	25.	I Chronicles 10-13
___	26.	Isaiah 58-60	___	26.	I Chronicles 14-16
___	27.	Isaiah 61-63	___	27.	I Chronicles 17-19
___	28.	Isaiah 64-66	___	28.	I Chronicles 20-23
___	29.	Micah 1-4	___	29.	I Chronicles 24-26
___	30.	Micah 5-7	___	30.	I Chronicles 27-29
___	31.	Nahum 1-3	___	31.	II Chronicles 1-3

(The Complete Schedule Continued)

September		October	
____ 1.	II Chronicles 4-6	____ 1.	Esther 4-7
____ 2.	II Chronicles 7-9	____ 2.	Esther 8-10
____ 3.	II Chronicles 10-13	____ 3.	Ezra 1-4
____ 4.	II Chronicles 14-16	____ 4.	Haggai 1-2/Zechariah 1-2
____ 5.	II Chronicles 17-19	____ 5.	Zechariah 1-2
____ 6.	II Chronicles 20-22	____ 6.	Zechariah 3-6
____ 7.	II Chronicles 23-25	____ 7.	Zechariah 7-10
____ 8.	II Chronicles 26-29	____ 8.	Ezra 5-7
____ 9.	II Chronicles 30-32	____ 9.	Ezra 8-10
____ 10.	II Chronicles 33-36	____ 10.	Nehemiah 1-3
____ 11.	Ezekiel 1-3	____ 11.	Nehemiah 4-6
____ 12.	Ezekiel 4-7	____ 12.	Nehemiah 7-9
____ 13.	Ezekiel 8-11	____ 13.	Nehemiah 10-13
____ 14.	Ezekiel 12-14	____ 14.	Malachi 1-4
____ 15.	Ezekiel 15-18	____ 15.	Matthew 1-4
____ 16.	Ezekiel 19-21	____ 16.	Matthew 5-7
____ 17.	Ezekiel 22-24	____ 17.	Matthew 8-11
____ 18.	Ezekiel 25-27	____ 18.	Matthew 12-15
____ 19.	Ezekiel 28-30	____ 19.	Matthew 16-19
____ 20.	Ezekiel 31-33	____ 20.	Matthew 20-22
____ 21.	Ezekiel 34-36	____ 21.	Matthew 23-25
____ 22.	Ezekiel 37-39	____ 22.	Matthew 26-28
____ 23.	Ezekiel 40-42	____ 23.	Mark 1-3
____ 24.	Ezekiel 43-45	____ 24.	Mark 4-6
____ 25.	Ezekiel 46-48	____ 25.	Mark 7-10
____ 26.	Daniel 1-3	____ 26.	Mark 11-13
____ 27.	Daniel 4-6	____ 27.	Mark 14-16
____ 28.	Daniel 7-9	____ 28.	Luke 1-3
____ 29.	Daniel 10-12	____ 29.	Luke 4-6
____ 30.	Esther 1-3	____ 30.	Luke 7-9
		____ 31.	Luke 10-13

(The Complete Schedule Continued)

November		**December**	
____ 1.	Luke 14-17	____ 1.	Romans 5-8
____ 2.	Luke 18-21	____ 2.	Romans 9-11
____ 3.	Luke 22-24	____ 3.	Romans 12-16
____ 4.	John 1-3	____ 4.	Acts 20:3-22
____ 5.	John 4-6	____ 5.	Acts 23-25
____ 6.	John 7-10	____ 6.	Acts 26-28
____ 7.	John 11-13	____ 7.	Ephesians 1-3
____ 8.	John 14-17	____ 8.	Ephesians 4-6
____ 9.	John 18-21	____ 9.	Philippians 1-4
____ 10.	Acts 1-2	____ 10.	Colossians 1-4
____ 11.	Acts 3-5	____ 11.	Hebrews 1-4
____ 12.	Acts 6-9	____ 12.	Hebrews 5-7
____ 13.	Acts 10-12	____ 13.	Hebrews 8-10
____ 14.	Acts 13-14	____ 14.	Hebrews 11-13
____ 15.	James 1-2	____ 15.	Philemon/I Peter 1-2
____ 16.	James 3-5	____ 16.	I Peter 3-5
____ 17.	Galatians 1-3	____ 17.	II Peter 1-3
____ 18.	Galatians 4-6	____ 18.	I Timothy 1-3
____ 19.	Acts 15-18:11	____ 19.	I Timothy 4-6
____ 20.	I Thessalonians 1-5	____ 20.	Titus 1-3
____ 21.	II Thessalonians 1-3	____ 21.	II Timothy 1-4
____ 22.	I Corinthians 1-4	____ 22.	I John 1-2; Acts 18:12-19:10
____ 23.	I John 3-5	____ 23.	I Corinthians 5-8
____ 24.	II John, III John	____ 24.	I Corinthians 9-12
____ 25.	Revelation 1-3, Jude	____ 25.	I Corinthians 13-16
____ 26.	Revelation 4-6	____ 26.	Acts 19:11-20:1; II Corinthians 1-3
____ 27.	Revelation 7-9	____ 27.	II Corinthians 4-6
____ 28.	Revelation 10-12	____ 28.	II Corinthians 7-9
____ 29.	Revelation 13-15	____ 29.	II Corinthians 10-13
____ 30.	Revelation 16-18	____ 30.	Acts 20:2/Romans 1-4
____ 31.	Revelation 19-22		

SELF-TEST

1. Write the Key Verse from memory.

   _____

   _____

   _____

2. How many books are in the Old Testament?

   _____

3. How many books are in the New Testament?

   _____

4. Why is it important to have a systematic plan for reading the Bible?

   _____

   _____

   _____

5. What were the four suggestions for successful Bible reading?

   _____

   _____

   _____

(Answers to tests are provided at the conclusion of the final chapter in this manual.)

FOR FURTHER STUDY

-Review the descriptions of each book of the Bible given in this chapter.
-Write the name of each book of the Bible below.
-By the name of each book summarize its basic content in three or four words.
-The first two are done as examples for you to follow.
(By condensing material in this manner you will be able to develop a general knowledge of the content of the entire Bible.)

Name Of Book	Content
Genesis	Book of beginnings
Exodus	Exit from Egypt

_____

_____

_____

_____

_____

_____

_____

_____

_____

_____

_____

_____

_____

_____

_____

_____

_____

_____

_____

_____

_____

_____

CHAPTER THREE

VERSIONS OF THE BIBLE

OBJECTIVES:

Upon completion of this chapter you will be able to:

- Write the Key Verse from memory.
- Name the three languages in which the Bible was written.
- Define the word "version."
- Explain the difference between a translation and a paraphrase version of the Bible.

KEY VERSE:

The Lord gave the Word: great was the company of those that published it. (Psalm 68:11)

INTRODUCTION

This chapter identifies the original languages in which the Bible was written and explains how the Scriptures have been translated into other languages. You will learn the difference between a translation and a paraphrase version of the Bible. Examples from various versions of the Bible are provided.

THREE LANGUAGES

The Bible was originally written in three languages. Most of the Old Testament was written in Hebrew except for parts of the books of Daniel and Nehemiah which were written in Aramaic. The New Testament was written in Greek.

None of the original manuscripts of the Bible are now in existence. Some good manuscripts exist which are copies of the original. Versions are translations of these copies of the original manuscripts. From early times men saw the necessity of translating the Bible so everyone could read it in their own language.

No translation is exact because no two languages are exactly alike. Some words used in the Bible do not even exist in different languages. For example, there is a tribe of Indians in Ecuador, South America, called the Auca Indians. When missionaries first contacted them, these Indians did not know how to read or write. There were no words in their language for "writing" or "book."

The Auca Indians did have a custom of carving identification marks on their property. Since there were no words in their language for scriptures, writing, or book, when the Bible was translated for them it was called "God's Carving." This identified it as something belonging to God. This is just one example of the difficulties in translating the Bible into various languages.

TRANSLATIONS AND PARAPHRASES

There are many different versions of the Bible. The word "version" means a Bible written in a language different from those in which God's Word was originally written. There are two main types of versions of the Bible: Translations and paraphrases.

TRANSLATION:

A translation is an effort to express what the Greek, Hebrew, and Aramaic words actually say. It gives as nearly as possible a literal word by word translation. Extra words are inserted only when it is necessary in order for the reader to understand the meaning.

PARAPHRASE:

A paraphrase does not attempt to translate word for word. It translates thought by thought. A paraphrase is a restatement of the meaning of a passage. Paraphrase versions are easier to read and understand because they are written in modern vocabulary and grammar, but they are not an exact translation of God's Word.

The "For Further Study" section of this chapter provides examples from several English versions of the Bible for you to compare. These illustrate the differences in translation and paraphrase versions.

SELECTING A STUDY BIBLE

For purposes of this course and Bible study in general, we recommend use of the King James version of the Bible. There are several reasons for this:

FIRST:

The King James Bible is very accurate and a good translation for serious study. A paraphrase version does not contain the exact word-by-word translation of Scriptures.

SECOND:

There are more study tools available for the King James version. There are a large number of concordances, dictionaries, and commentaries written for the King James text.

THIRD:

The King James version is available in more languages than any other version. Since Harvestime International Institute courses are used throughout the world, we selected this version of the Bible because it is available in many languages. It is important to have a Bible in your native tongue because you think and understand best in your own language.

If you do not have a King James version of the Bible write to the American Bible Society at P.O. Box 5601, Grand Central Station, New York, New York 10164, U.S.A. They have a complete listing of all the languages in which the King James version of the Bible is available. If you find the King James Version is not available in your language or have difficulty in obtaining a Bible, write to the United Bible Societies, Bible House, P.O. Box 755, Stuttgart 1, Germany. They maintain a list of "Scriptures of the World" which identifies all the languages in the world in which at least one book of the Bible has been published.

If you read English but have a limited vocabulary, you may be interested in obtaining the "Bible in Basic English." This is the entire Old and New Testament written in English using only a basic 1,000 word vocabulary. Write to Cambridge University Press, New York, New York, U.S.A. for further information.

RED LETTER EDITIONS

Several versions of the Bible come in what are called "red letter editions." In red letter editions of the Bible the words of Jesus are printed in red. The rest of the text of the Bible is printed in black ink.

If a red letter edition of the King James version is available in your language, we suggest you obtain it. What Jesus taught is one of the major focuses of Harvestime International Institute training and a red-letter edition emphasizes His teachings.

A SUMMARY

The following chart summarizes how the various versions of the Bible developed:

> The Bible:
> Inspired By God
>
> |
>
> Revealed To Holy Men Who Wrote God's Words
> In Greek, Hebrew, Aramaic
>
> |
>
> Interpreted Into Various Languages
> Resulting In
>
> |
>
> Exact Translations And Paraphrase Versions Of The Bible

SELF-TEST

1. Write the Key Verse from memory.

_____

_____

_____

2. What does the word "version" mean?

_____

3. What is the difference between a translation and a paraphrase version of the Bible?

_____

_____

4. What version of the Bible is used in this course?

_____

5. Why is no translation of the Bible exact?

_____

_____

6. What are the three languages in which the Bible was originally written?

_____

_____

_____

(Answers to tests are provided at the conclusion of the final chapter in this manual.)

FOR FURTHER STUDY

We have selected the text of John 3:16 to illustrate the difference between the different versions of the Bible. The versions listed are the most popular English versions of the Bible.

King James Version: For God so loved the world that He gave his only begotten Son that whosoever believeth in Him should not perish but have everlasting life.

New King James Version: For God so loved the world that He gave His only begotten Son, that whoever believes in Him should not perish but have everlasting life.

Revised Standard Version: For God so loved the world that He gave His only Son, that whoever believes in Him should not perish but have eternal life.

Living Bible: For God loved the world so much that He gave His only Son so that anyone who believes in Him shall not perish but have eternal life.

New American Standard Bible: For God so loved the world, that He gave His only begotten Son, that whoever believes in Him should not perish, but have eternal life.

New English Bible: God loved the world so much that He gave His only Son, that everyone who has faith in Him may not die but have eternal life.

Amplified Version: For God so greatly loved and dearly prized the world that He (even) gave up His only-begotten (unique) Son, so that whoever believes in (trusts, clings to, relies on) Him shall not perish-come to destruction, be lost-but have eternal (everlasting) life.

Phillips: For God loved the world so much that He gave His only Son, so that everyone who believes in Him should not be lost, but should have eternal life.

Wurst: For in such a manner did God love the world, insomuch that His Son, the uniquely-begotten One, He gave, in order that everyone who places his trust in Him may not perish but may be having life eternal.

Moffat: For God loved the world so dearly that He gave up His only Son, so that everyone who believes in Him may have eternal life instead of perishing.

CHAPTER FOUR

BEFORE YOU BEGIN

OBJECTIVES:

Upon completion of this chapter you will be able to:

• Write the Key Verse from memory.
• Identify prerequisites to effective Bible study.
• Identify two ways God provided for studying His Word.
• Recognize the teaching ministry of the Holy Spirit.
• Explain the difference between the milk and meat of the Word of God.
• Identify three steps for moving from the milk to the meat of the Word of God.
• List three practical suggestions for studying God's Word.

KEY VERSE:

He that is of God heareth God's words: ye therefore hear them not, because ye are not of God. (John 8:47)

INTRODUCTION

Many people try to begin Bible study the same way they study any other book. They take their Bible, open it, and start to read. But often their study does not last long. They find it difficult to understand what they read. They do not recognize how the Bible relates to everyday living and may even think it is a rather dull book. The Bible explains that only certain people will be able to understand God's Word. People fail at Bible study because they are not spiritually prepared to study the Word of God.

The Bible is like a door which leads into the presence of God. Behind that door are great spiritual treasures. But you must have the key to unlock the door or you will never be able to enter in and explore these treasures. The Bible reveals how to understand God's Word. It provides the key to unlock the door to spiritual understanding.

PREREQUISITES TO BIBLE STUDY

A prerequisite is something you must do before you can do something else. The Bible is the Word of God. It is not like any other book and you cannot study it as you do other books. There are prerequisites--things you must do before you can begin--if you are to understand the deep spiritual things of God.

If you want to understand the Bible you must first know the Author of the Bible. Jesus said:

> **He that is of God heareth God's words: ye therefore hear them not, because ye are not of God. (John 8:47)**

You cannot understand God's Words without knowing God. How do you come to know God? Jesus told Nicodemus, who was a religious leader in the nation of Israel:

> **Verily, verily, I say unto thee, Except a man be born again he cannot see the kingdom of God. (John 3:3)**

A man may be educated, learned, cultured, and even religious, but the understanding of Scripture will be hidden from him until his spiritual eyes have been opened by the new birth.

Nicodemus asked Jesus, "How can these things be?" He did not understand what Jesus meant. Jesus answered and said:

> **Art thou a master of Israel, and knowest not these things? (John 3:10)**

Nicodemus was a religious leader of Israel, yet he did not know about being born again. In fact, he asked . . .

> **How can a man be born when he is old? can he enter the second time into his mother's womb, and be born? (John 3:4)**

Jesus explained to Nicodemus that the new birth of which He was speaking was a spiritual birth. This new birth experience comes through faith in Jesus Christ. You must confess you are a sinner. You must believe Jesus died for your sins, ask forgiveness for your sins, and accept Him as your personal Savior.

The person who has not been born again cannot receive the truth of God's Words:

> **But the natural man receiveth not the things of the Spirit of God: for they are foolishness unto him; neither can he know them, because they are spiritually discerned. (I Corinthians 2:14)**

The unsaved man may admire the Bible for its literary beauty and value. He may study it historically or geographically. But the spiritual truths of God's Word will remain hidden until he receives forgiveness of sin:

> **For the preaching of the cross is to them that perish foolishness; but unto us which are saved it is the power of God. (I Corinthians 1:18)**

GOD'S PROVISIONS

From the moment you accept Jesus as your Savior and experience the new spiritual birth, your mind will begin to understand spiritual truths in God's Word. Just as a new born baby in the natural world needs physical nourishment from food, a person who is spiritually reborn needs nourishment. Their food for this spiritual growth and development is the Word of God.   There are two ways God has provided to help you study His Word:

TEACHERS:

God chooses certain believers as leaders in the Church. One of the special leadership positions is that of being a teacher of God's Word:

> **And God hath set some in the church, first apostles, secondarily prophets, thirdly teachers . . . (I Corinthians 12:28)**
>
> **And He gave some apostles; and some, prophets; and some, evangelists; and some, pastors, and teachers;**
>
> **For the perfecting of the saints, for the work of the ministry, for the edifying of the body of Christ;**
>
> **Till we all come in the unity of the faith, and of the knowledge of the Son of God, unto a perfect man, unto the measure of the stature of the fullness of Christ. (Ephesians 4:11-13)**

God provides teachers to explain God's Word and guide you to spiritual maturity.

A SPECIAL TEACHER:

God has a second way for you to learn His Word. He commands you to study it yourself:

> **Study to show thyself approved unto God, a workman that needeth not to be ashamed, rightly dividing the Word of truth. (II Timothy 2:15)**

God has provided a special Teacher to help you when you study His Word.   When Jesus was living on earth He personally taught His followers the truths of God. But Jesus knew that after His death and resurrection He would be returning to Heaven so He told His followers that a special Teacher would be sent to help them understand God's Word. That Teacher is the Holy Spirit:

> **But the comforter, which is the Holy Ghost, whom the Father will send in my name, He shall teach you all things, and bring all things to your remembrance, whatsoever I have said unto you. (John 14:26)**

> **Howbeit when He, the Spirit of truth is come, He will guide you into all truth; for He shall not speak of Himself; but whatsoever He shall hear, that shall He speak and He will shew you things to come. (John 16:13)**

The coming of the Holy Spirit is recorded in Acts chapter 2. Read this chapter in your Bible. God wants you to experience this same infilling of the Holy Spirit.* Through the Holy Spirit you receive a special ability from God to understand His Word:

> **But the anointing which ye have received of Him abideth in you, and ye need not that any man teach you; but as the same anointing teacheth you of all things and is truth, and is no lie, and even as it hath taught you, ye shall abide in Him. (I John 2:27)**

The Holy Spirit is a creative power. It was the Spirit of God that breathed into man the breath of life (Genesis 2:7). It was that same Spirit that raised Jesus from the dead. (Romans 8:11). It is that creative power of the Holy Spirit that takes ordinary study and turns it into CREATIVE study of God's Word.

We said in the introduction to this course that to be creative is to produce something new. The teaching of the Holy Spirit produces a new flow of spiritual understanding. The Holy Spirit makes the Bible new, fresh, and relevant to your life.

GOD'S WORD: MILK AND MEAT

There are two levels of spiritual depth in God's Word. We call these the "milk" level and the "meat" levels. The "milk" of God's Word refers to simple truths that even a child can understand, such as the plan of salvation. The "meat" of God's Word refers to deeper spiritual truths which are not so easy to understand.

---

* If you have not received the infilling of the Holy Spirit, order the Harvestime International Institute course *"Ministry Of The Holy Spirit."*

Some people have received Jesus as their Savior and been filled with the Holy Spirit, but they do not seem to grow in their understanding of God's Word. They are still feeding on the milk of the Word.

In the natural world there is nothing wrong with milk for a newborn baby. The same is true in the spiritual world. When you are first born again you should desire the milk of God's Word:

> **As newborn babes, desire the sincere milk of the word, that ye may grow thereby. (I Peter 2:2)**

But there comes a time in the natural world that a baby must start to eat solid foods if he is to mature physically. This is also true in the spiritual world. There is a time when you must move on from the milk of God's Word to the meat:

> **For every one that useth milk is unskillful in the word of righteousness; for he is a babe.**

> **But strong meat belongeth to them that are of full age, even those who by reason and use have their senses exercised to discern both good and evil. (Hebrews 5:13-14)**

Paul said that when it was time for believers to move from spiritual milk to meat, some were not ready:

> **For when for the time ye ought to be teachers, ye have need that one teach you again which be the first principles of the oracles of God; and are become such as have need of milk, and not of strong meat. (Hebrews 5:12)**

Why was this so? Why is it that some believers go deep into God's Word while others never get beyond a surface understanding of the Bible? Why are some people always hungering for "deeper things" in God's Word instead of experiencing them? Paul wrote:

> **And I brethren, could not speak unto you as unto spiritual, but as unto carnal, even as unto babes in Christ.**

> **I have fed you with milk, and not with meat; for hitherto ye were not able to bear it, neither yet now are ye able.**

> **For ye are yet carnal: for whereas there is among you envying, and strife, and divisions, are ye not carnal, and walk as men? (I Corinthians 3:1-3)**

They could not move from milk to meat because they were carnal Christians. This means they were spiritually immature. They had envy, strife, division, and other sins in their lives. When a Christian is carnal, he will not be able to understand the deeper truths of God's Word. He will remain on milk until he repents and grows up enough spiritually that he can digest meat.

It is God's desire that you move from the milk to the meat of His Word. This is how you increase your knowledge of God's Word:

> **Whom shall He teach knowledge? And who shall be made to understand doctrine? Them that are weaned from the milk and drawn from the breasts. (Isaiah 28:9)**

It is important that you move from the milk to the meat for it is upon spiritually mature believers that God pours out His Spirit:

> **Whom shall He teach knowledge? and whom shall He make to understand doctrine? them that are weaned from the milk and drawn from the breasts.**

> **For precept must be upon precept, precept upon precept; line upon line, line upon line; here a little, and there a little;**

> **For with stammering lips and another tongue will He speak to this people.**

> **To whom He said, This is the rest wherewith ye may cause the weary to rest; and this is the refreshing: yet they would not hear. (Isaiah 28:9-12)**

God wanted to bless His people with an outpouring of the Holy Spirit. He wanted to revive them and give them spiritual rest, but they could not enter in because they had not heard His Words. They could not move on to spiritual meat because they were not weaned from the milk of the Word.

HOW TO MOVE FROM MILK TO MEAT

Now, the big question is . . . How does a newborn Christian move from the milk to the meat of God's Word?

DESIRE THE MILK:

First, you must desire the milk of the Word. You must gain an understanding of the basic principles of the Word of God:

> **As newborn babes, desire the sincere milk of the word that ye may grow thereby. (I Peter 2:2)**

You cannot start with spiritual meat. You must first desire and learn to digest spiritual milk.

BE OBEDIENT TO GOD'S WORD:

This is the most important step. Carnal Christians do not obey what they learn in the milk God's Word so they are not able to mature on to meat. The Bible teaches that it is not enough to hear His Word. You must be obedient. You must become a "doer" of the Word and not a "hearer" only:

> **But be ye doers of the word, and not hearers only, deceiving your own selves. (James 1:22)**

An increase in spiritual understanding comes through meditation on and obedience to God's Word. This is how we move from milk to meat. David wrote:

> **Thou through thy commandments hast made me wiser than mine enemies. . . I have more understanding than all my teachers: for thy testimonies are my meditation.**
>
> **I understand more than the ancients, because I keep thy precepts . . .Through thy precepts I get understanding: Therefore I hate every false way . . . (Portions of Psalm 119:99-104)**

Because David kept God's precepts and was a doer of the Word, his understanding increased. God will not take you on to the deeper revelations if you have not acted upon what you have learned in the milk of the Word.

SEARCH FOR THE MEAT:

In the natural world, chewing meat requires more physical effort than drinking milk. The same is true in the spiritual world. Discovering the meat of God's Word requires more spiritual effort than living on the milk of the Word.

Proverbs chapter 2 tells how to search for the meat:

> **My son, if thou wilt receive my words, and hide my commandments with thee;**
>
> **So that thou incline thine ear unto wisdom, and apply thine heart to understanding;**
>
> **Yea, if thou criest after knowledge, and liftest up thy voice for understanding;**
>
> **If you seekest her as silver and searchest for her as for hid treasures:**

Then shalt thou understand the fear of the Lord and find the knowledge of God. (Proverbs 2:1-5)

These are the steps to discovering and understanding the knowledge of God:

1. Receive my words: You must be teachable.

2. Hide my commandments with thee: You must accept the Word and integrate it into your life and spirit. Do not try to change the Word to agree with your way of living.

3. Incline thine ear unto wisdom: Really listen to what God is saying to you through His Word. Listening requires changes in living where indicated.

4. Apply thine heart to understanding: Apply yourself diligently to understanding (interpreting) the Word.

5. Seek her as silver and search for her as for hid treasures: If someone told you there was a hidden treasure in property you own, what would you do? You would start digging. You would conduct a systematic search until you found the treasure. It would become a priority of your life.

When you make God's Word a priority and begin to systematically search for His wisdom, you will find it. But it must become a priority of life. You must approach it with as much excitement and dedication as if you were searching for treasure.

If you follow these guidelines and search for the meat of God`s Word, these are the results:

1. Then shalt thou understand the fear of the Lord: Verse 5

2. And find the knowledge of God: Verse 5

3. Then shalt thou understand righteousness, and judgment, and equity; yea every good path: Verse 9

4. It will be pleasant unto thy soul: (You will find satisfaction) Verse 10

5. Discretion shall preserve thee: Discretion is the ability to make sound judgment and decisions. Verse 11

6. Understanding shall keep thee: Verse 11

7. You will be delivered from all evil: Verse 12

SOME PRACTICAL SUGGESTIONS

Here are some practical suggestions for Bible study.

SET A SPECIAL TIME:

Set a special time each day when you will study. The time you select will depend on your personal schedule or preference. Some prefer to study early in the morning when they are fresh and rested. Some find their best time to be late at night when everyone else in their household has retired. Whatever time you select, set it apart as a regular appointment time with God to study His Word.

SELECT A SPECIAL PLACE:

Select a place that is as free from noise and interruption as possible. Be sure to have good lighting to enable you to read without eye strain. If it is possible, select a place where you can leave your study materials, i.e., Bible, pencil, paper, and any Bible study books you may have. This way you do not have to spend time each day collecting these items before you start your study.

START A SPECIAL WAY:

Start each study session with prayer. Ask God to open your understanding so you will be able to receive His Word. The Psalmist David prayed:

> **Let my cry come near before thee, O Lord; give me understanding according to thy Word. (Psalm 119:169)**

SELF-TEST

1. Write the Key Verse from memory.

_____

_____

_____

2. Why do many people fail when they start studying the Bible?

_____

_____

3. What does the word "prerequisite" mean?

_____

_____

4. What is the key prerequisite for understanding the Bible?

_____

_____

5. List two ways God has provided for you to study His Word.

_____

_____

6. Who was the great Teacher sent from God after Jesus returned to Heaven?

_____

7. What is meant by the "milk " of the Word of God?

_____

_____

8. What is meant by the "meat" of the Word of God?

_____

_____

9. List three steps that move a believer from the milk to the meat of the Word of God:

_____

_____

_____

10. List three practical suggestions for Bible study which were discussed in this chapter:

_____

_____

_____

(Answers to tests are provided at the conclusion of the final chapter in this manual.)

FOR FURTHER STUDY

1. Turn to I Corinthians 3:1-3 in your Bible. List three words Paul used to describe carnal Christians.

_____

_____

_____

2. From Proverbs 2: 1-5, list five steps given for searching for the meat of God's Word.

_____

_____

_____

_____

3. Study Proverbs 2:5-12. List seven results of applying these steps to the study of God's Word.

_____

_____

_____

_____

_____

_____

_____

CHAPTER FIVE

BIBLE STUDY TOOLS

OBJECTIVES:

Upon completion of this chapter you will be able to:

- Write the Key Verses from memory.
- Explain three uses of a concordance.
- Use a concordance.
- Use a Bible dictionary.
- Use a Bible word study book.
- Use a topical textbook.
- Use a Bible encyclopedia.
- Use a Bible commentary.
- Use a Bible atlas.
- Use a Bible handbook.

KEY VERSES:

Thou through thy commandments hast made me wiser than mine enemies: for they are ever with me.

I have more understanding than all my teachers: for thy testimonies are my meditation.

I understand more than the ancients, because I keep thy precepts.
(Psalm 119:98-100)

INTRODUCTION

Bible scholars have written special books that are helpful in studying the Bible. This chapter explains how to use these Bible study tools. It is not necessary to have these special books in order to study the Bible. Do not be concerned if you cannot afford or do not have access to them. This course teaches you how to study the Bible yourself. All that is necessary for you to have is a Bible.

If you <u>do not</u> have these tools at the present time, it is still important for you to know what study aids exist. This is why we have included this chapter on Bible study tools. If you <u>do</u> have access to Bible study tools, we want you to know how to use them because they will be helpful to you.

There are several ways you might gain access to such books. Perhaps you can obtain them by purchasing them at a Christian bookstore or from the publisher. If you cannot afford to purchase these books, perhaps you can borrow them. If you live near a Christian Bible college, you might be able to use their library. Perhaps a minister or Christian friend living near you has some of these books and will let you use them.

Bible study tools are important, but they cannot substitute for studying the Bible itself. You should use these tools only after you have done your own study of the Word. Consulting a Bible study book before studying the Bible itself influences your mind with the comments of man before you have studied the words of God. Those who wrote Bible commentaries and other study tools obtained their material the way any student can get it: From the Bible itself.

It is not necessary to depend on the research of others. If Bible study tools are not available to you, do not despair. Within you dwells the creative power of the Holy Spirit. He is the special teacher sent by God who will guide you into all truth. That is better than all the Bible study tools provided by men. If these tools are available, learn to use them to supplement your own study of God's Word, but do not depend on them. Depend on the creative revelation of the Holy Spirit.

BIBLE CONCORDANCE

A Bible concordance provides an alphabetical listing of the main words in the Bible with the immediate context of each word. If you have limited funds with which to purchase materials, this is the most important tool for Bible study and should be your first choice.

Two good concordances are:

> The Analytical Concordance to the Bible by Robert Young published by Eerdmans Publishing Company, Grand Rapids, Michigan, U.S.A.

> Exhaustive Concordance of the Bible by James Strong published by Abingdon Press, Nashville, Tennessee, U.S.A. (Strong's is used for the following study explaining the use of a concordance.)

A concordance is helpful in three ways:

1. To Locate All The References To A Word:

For example, if you want to study about angels you can look up the words "angel" and "angels" in a concordance. You will find a complete listing of each place these words are used in the Bible. This will enable you to look up each reference on the subject. You can also look up names of Bible characters and do biographical studies using the concordance. For example, if you look up the name "Moses" it lists all of the Bible references to him.

Each reference to a word is represented by the first letter of the word. For example, look at the listing for the word "begotten":

BEGOTTEN

b Seth were eight hundred years	Gen 5:4	3205
b of thy father, she is thy	Lev 18:11	4138
have I b them that thou	Num 11:12	3205
The children that are b of them	Deut 23 8	3205
and then sons of his body b	Judg 8:30	3318
or who hath b the drops of dew	Job 38:28	3205
this day have I b thee	Ps 2:7	3205
thine heart, Who hath b me these	Is 49:21	3205
for they have b strange children	Hos 5:7	3205
as of the only b of the Father	Jn 1:13	3439
the only b Son, which is in the	Jn 1:18	3439
that he gave his only b Son	Jn 3:16	3439
the name of the only b Son of God	Jn 3:18	3439
my Son, this day have I b thee	Acts 13:33	1080

The word "begotten" is indicated by the initial "b" in each reference listed. Abbreviations are used for the books of the Bible rather than spelling out the name of each book.

2. To Locate A Specific Text:

Perhaps you remember just a word or two from a Bible verse and you want to find the verse in the Bible. Use the words you remember to locate the text. For example, if you remember the word "begotten" from the verse "For God so loved the world He gave His only begotten Son," you can look up the word "begotten" in the concordance. There you will find all the references to "begotten" listed. Go down the list until you find the verse you are looking for . . . "God so loved the world that He gave His only begotten Son." By using the concordance you discovered that this verse is located in John 3:16. Now you can find the verse in your Bible.

3. To Find The Meaning Of A Word:

At the end of each listing under a word in the concordance you will find a number. In the back of the concordance there are two dictionaries. One dictionary is in Hebrew, the language in which the Old Testament was written. The other dictionary is in Greek, the language in which the New Testament was written. You do not need to know Hebrew or Greek to use these dictionaries. Use the number which is at the end of the listing in the concordance:

Jo 3:16 that he gave his only b son. . . 3439

57

Look up the number in the Hebrew dictionary if it is a word used in the Old Testament. Look up the number in the Greek dictionary if it is a word used in the New Testament. We are studying the word "begotten" as it is used in John 3:16. Since it is a New Testament word we will look up number 3439 in the Greek dictionary. This is how the listing in the Greek dictionary looks:

```
 (1)      (2)        (3)          (4)
3439 Hoyoyevhs  monogenes, mon-og-en-ace';
      (5)                        (6)
from  3441 and 1096; only-born, i.e., sole-only begotten child.
```

The numbers in brackets ( ) do not appear in the dictionary. These are coded to the following explanations:

(1)   This is the number by which you find the Greek word.

(2)   This is the word written in Greek.

(3)   This shows how the word is pronounced in Greek.

(4)   This shows the division of the word into syllables (parts) and where the accent (emphasis) is placed when you say the word in Greek.

(5)   This provides the numbers of the "root" words for the word "begotten." These are the original words from which the word "begotten" came. (You can look these up in the Greek dictionary too if you desire. Look them up by their numbers).

(6)   This gives the meaning of the word "begotten."

When you do not understand the meaning of a word in the Bible this method of word study will help you. You will learn more about word study later in this course.

BIBLE DICTIONARY

A Bible dictionary lists words of the Bible in alphabetical order and explains the meaning of each word. A Bible dictionary is not the same as a regular word dictionary. A regular dictionary gives the meanings of words as they are now used. A Bible dictionary gives the definitions of Bible words as they were used in the original context of Scripture. Here is a sample listing from a Bible dictionary:

BEARD (berd), with Asiatics a badge of manly dignity in contrast to the Egyptians, who usually shaved the head and the face. As a sign of mourning, it was the custom to pluck it out or cut it off. The Israelites were forbidden to shave off the corners of the beards, probably because it was regarded as a heathenish sign (Lev. 19:27). To compel a man to cut off his beard was to inflict upon him a shameful disgrace (II Sam. 10:4)

The following are recommended Bible dictionaries:

Unger's Bible Dictionary by Merrill Unger. Published by Moody Press, Chicago, Illinois, U.S.A.

Zondervan Pictorial Bible Dictionary by Merrill C. Tenney published by Zondervan Publishing House, Grand Rapids, Michigan, U.S.A.

WORD STUDY BOOKS

Word study books go beyond the basic Bible dictionary in defining words used in the Bible. They provide the Greek or Hebrew word and various meanings given to the same word. A word study book also provides the references in a which word is used. Here is an example from a word study book:

AXE: From AXINE, an axe, kin to agumi, to break,

is found in Matthew 3:10 and Luke 3:9

This listing shows the Greek Word, tells it is related to another word ("agumi"), explains the meaning of the word, and tells where the word is used in the Bible.

The following word study books are suggested:

An Expository Dictionary of New Testament Words and An Expository Dictionary of Old Testament words, both by W.E. Vine published by Fleming H. Revell Company, Old Tappan, New Jersey, U.S.A.

BIBLE ENCYCLOPEDIA

A Bible encyclopedia also lists various Bible subjects and words in alphabetical order and defines them. But it provides a more extensive discussion than a dictionary.

Here is an example from a Bible encyclopedia:

> BEGOTTEN Heb. Yalad (Lev. 18:11; Job 38:28; Psalm 2:7; etc.); Gk. Yennao (Acts 13:33; Hebrews 1:5; 5:5).; NEB also "sired), "become your father", etc. In the RSV the term occurs mainly of God's act in making Christ His Son: "You are my son; today I have begotten you" (Psalm 2:7), quoted in Acts 13:33 in reference to His resurrection (Rom 1:4). The same passage is cited in Heb 1:5 as proving Christ's filial dignity, transcending the angels in that "the name he has obtained is more excellent then theirs," i.e., the name of son; and again (5:5) of God's conferring upon Christ the glory of the priestly office.

The following are recommended Bible Encyclopedias:

Wycliffe Bible Encyclopedia by C.F. Pfeiffer, V.F. Vos, and John Rea; published by Moody Press, Chicago, Illinois, U.S.A.

The Zondervan Pictorial Encyclopedia, (five volumes) published by Zondervan Publishing House, Grand Rapids, Michigan, U.S.A.

BIBLE COMMENTARY

A commentary is a book that provides comments about Scriptures in the Bible. It comments on the Bible chapter by chapter and verse by verse. A commentary is helpful in explaining passages which are difficult to understand. But remember: This is one person's ideas as to what the Scriptures mean. Commentaries are only opinions of man. This is why it is important that you study the Bible for yourself and not depend only on the comments of others.

There are many different Bible commentaries. Some commentaries consist of one volume which covers the entire Bible. Other commentaries devote one book of comments to each book of the Bible. Suggested commentaries:

The Wycliff Bible Commentary by Charles F. Pfeiffer and Everett F. Harrison published in by Moody Press, Chicago, Illinois, U.S.A.

Matthew Henry's Commentary of the Whole Bible published by Zondervan Publishing House, Grand Rapids, Michigan, U.S.A.

BIBLE ATLAS

A Bible atlas or geography contains maps and information on the lands of the Bible. It helps you locate and understand the geographical setting in which the incidents in the Bible happened. The following atlases are recommended:

Compact Bible Atlas with Gazetter published by Baker Book House, Grand Rapids, Michigan, U.S.A.

Hammond's Atlas of the Bible Lands by Harry T. Frank published by Scripture Press, Wheaton, Illinois, U.S.A.

Oxford Bible Atlas by Herbert G. May published by Oxford University Press, New York, New York, U.S.A.

The Macmillan Bible Atlas published by Macmillan Publishing Company, New York, New York, U.S.A.

TOPICAL TEXTBOOKS

A topical textbook is a book which organizes the Bible under major topical listings and gives the verses where these topics are discussed. Here is an example from a topical textbook:

GIDEON. Call of by an angel, Judg. 6:11,14. His excuses, Judg. 6:15. Promises of the Lord to, Judg. 6:16. Angel attests the call to, by miracle, Judg. 6:21-24. He destroys the altar of Baal, and builds one to the Lord, Judg. 6:25-27. His prayer tests, Judg. 6:36-40. Leads an army against and defeats the Midianites, Judg. 6:33-35; 7; 8:4-12. Ephriamites chide, for not inviting them to join in the campaign against Midianites, Judg. 8:1-3. Avenges himself upon the people of Succoth, Judg. 8:14-17. Israel desires to make him king, he refuses, Judg. 8;22-23. Makes an ephod which becomes a snare to the Israelites, Judg. 8:24-27. Had seventy sons, Judg. 8:30. Death of, Judge 8:32; Faith of, Heb. 11:32

The following are recommended topical books:

Nave's Topical Bible lists 20,000 topics with 100,000 Bible references. It was written by Orville J. Nave and published by Guardian Press, Grand Rapids, Michigan, U.S.A.

Zondervan Topical Bible lists 21,000 topics with over 100,000 Scripture references published by Zondervan Publishing House, Grand Rapids, Michigan, U.S.A.

BIBLE HANDBOOKS

A Bible handbook is usually a one volume summary of selected information about the Bible. It contains helpful maps and charts, definitions, information on Bible times, and summaries of the books of the Bible. A Bible handbook presents a general overview of the Bible.

The following are good Bible handbooks:

Unger's Bible Handbook, Moody Press, Chicago, Illinois, U.S.A.

Eerdman's Handbook To The Bible, Eerdmans Publishing Company, Grand Rapids, Michigan, U.S.A.

INTERNET

For those who are computer literate and have access to the Internet, it is a wonderful resource for Bible study tools. Many of the study tools mentioned in this chapter can now be accessed via the Internet. Input the key words "Bible study resources" or "Bible studies." You may also input the title of the study aid you are seeking. For example, "Nave's Topical Bible" will locate this resource for you.

1. Write the Key Verses from memory.

_____

_____

_____

2. What are the three main uses of a concordance?

_____   _____   _____

3. Look at the words in List One, then look at the definitions in List Two. Write the number of the definition which best describes the word on the blank in front of it.

List One   **List Two**

___Topical textbook   1. Provides comments on the Bible, verse by verse, chapter by
                                             chapter.

___Bible dictionary   2. Like a regular dictionary, but defines words as they are used
                                             in the Bible rather than modern times.

___Bible encyclopedia   3. Provides maps and information on the geographical setting of
                                             the Bible.

___Commentary   4. Lists topics of the Bible and scriptural references for them.

___Bible atlas   5. Provides explanation for words in more detail than a Bible
                                             dictionary.

___Word study books   6. Provides general information on the Bible: Background, history,
                                             etc.

(Answers to tests are provided at the conclusion of the final chapter in this manual.)

FOR FURTHER STUDY

If you have access to Bible study tools, complete the following exercises:

1. Use a concordance to locate the following verse. Complete the verse and record the Bible reference:

"For there are certain men crept in unawares, who were before of old ordained to this

condemnation _____ ”

Reference:_____

2. Use the concordance, a Bible dictionary, and a word study book to study the word "lasciviousness." Summarize its meaning:

_____

_____

_____

3. Look up Jude 1:4 in a Bible commentary and see what comments are made about this verse. Summarize what you learn:

_____

_____

_____

_____

CHAPTER SIX

PRINCIPLES OF INTERPRETATION

OBJECTIVES:

Upon completion of this chapter you will be able to:

- Write the Key Verse from memory.
- Explain what it means to "rightly divide" the Word of truth.
- List six rules for properly interpreting the Bible.
- Define each of these six rules.
- Define verbal and plenary inspiration.

KEY VERSE:

Study to show thyself approved unto God, a workman that needeth not to be ashamed, rightly dividing the word of truth. (II Timothy 2:15)

INTRODUCTION

Read the Key Verse again. "Rightly dividing" as used here is taken from the rules for Old Testament sacrifices and means to "cut straight." In the Old Testament, when a person brought a sacrifice for sin, the animal was divided into three parts. One part was offered to God. Another part was given to the one who brought the offering. The third part went to the priest. From this practice the expression "rightly dividing" developed. It means to "give to each that which belongs to him."

In Bible study it is important to rightly divide the Word of God. This means you must understand what is being said to whom. You must also interpret and apply the meaning correctly.

There are three major groups to which the Word addresses itself. These are listed in I Corinthians 10:32:

Give none offense, neither to the Jews, nor to the Gentiles, nor to the Church of God. (I Corinthians 10:32)

All Scriptures were given FOR us, but not all verses are directed TO us. For example, God told Noah to build an ark. The story is recorded as an example from which you are to learn spiritual truths but it does not mean YOU should build an ark. Some of the Bible is directed to the Jews. Portions are directed to the Gentiles (nations other than the Jews). Other portions are directed to the Church (all those who are true believers in Jesus Christ).

In order to find the correct meaning from the Bible you must learn to rightly divide it. Another word for this is "interpretation" which means to give something proper meaning. You must learn how to arrive at the proper meaning for each Scripture. Jesus pointed out to the religious leaders of His time:

> **. . . Ye do err, not knowing the Scriptures nor the power of God.**
> **(Matthew 22:29)**

Spiritual error results from not knowing God's Word. There are certain principles you must follow in order to properly interpret the Bible. There are six basic rules for interpreting the Bible which help to "rightly divide" the Word of God.

THE RULE OF DIVINE AUTHORITY

The rule of divine authority means that we accept the Bible as the final authority. We believe that all the Bible is inspired by God, from Genesis through Revelation:

> **All Scripture is given by inspiration of God, and is profitable for doctrine, for reproof, for correction, for instruction in righteousness.**
> **(II Timothy 3:16)**

> **For the prophecy came not in old time by the will of man; but holy men of God spake as they were moved by the Holy Ghost. (II Peter 1:19-21)**

There are two different types of inspiration: Verbal and plenary inspiration.

By _verbal_ inspiration we mean that every word in the original manuscripts was inspired by God. By _plenary_ inspiration we mean full inspiration of all Scripture as opposed to partial inspiration. Every portion of the Bible is inspired.

When we accept the rule of divine authority, then there is no conflict between the Bible and history or science. If there is an apparent conflict it is because:

1. We have failed to understand science or history.

   or else. . .

2. The current scientific knowledge is not accurate. When conflicts are apparent, the Bible is taken as the final authority because it is the divinely inspired Word of God. In the past, when apparent conflicts between the Bible and history or science arose, later investigations always proved the Bible to be correct.

THE RULE OF LITERAL INTERPRETATION

To interpret the Bible literally means to believe it means exactly what it says. Always interpret the Bible literally unless the context clearly indicates otherwise.   When the Bible says Israel crossed the Jordan River on dry ground, accept it literally. When the Bible tells about the walls of Jericho falling down, accept it as it is recorded by the Holy Spirit.

The Bible does contain various "types." Certain persons, places, or events, while literal in themselves, also represent something that will happen in the future. Chapter Twenty-One of this course will help you recognize these.

Symbols are also used in the Bible. A symbol stands for a meaning in addition to its ordinary one. For example, in Mark 14:22 the wine is used as a symbol of the blood of the Lord Jesus Christ. (They were not drinking actual blood.)   Symbols are often used in Bible prophecy. For example the great image of which Nebuchadnezzar dreamed in Daniel has symbolic significance. Each part of the image represented a future world kingdom (Daniel 2). The Bible usually explains symbols when they are used. For example, Daniel's interpretation of the symbolic image is recorded in Daniel 2:31-45.

Jesus often used parables when He taught. A parable is a story that is told for the purpose of illustrating a spiritual truth. Whenever Jesus used a parable it is always stated in the Bible. If it does not say it was a parable then the story should be accepted as an actual event.

THE RULE OF CONTEXTUAL CONSIDERATION

Every verse of the Bible should be studied in its context. This means it should be studied in relation to the verses which precede and follow it, as well as in relation to the rest of the Bible. Many false doctrines and cults have been created because verses or parts of verses were taken out of their context.

For example, the Bible says there is no God. Did you know that? You will find this in Psalm 14:1. Right there it says "there is no God." But if we read all the passage then we have this:

The fool hath said in his heart, There is no God. (Psalm 14:1)

The complete verse in its context is quite different in meaning than the portion removed from the context.

To study a verse in its context ask yourself the following questions:

1. Who Is Speaking Or Writing?

Although all the Bible is God's Word, different men were used in writing and speaking it.

2. What Is Being Said?

Summarize the main points of what is being said by the speaker or writer.

3. To Whom Is It Being Said?

Israel? The Gentile nations? The Church? A specific individual?

4. Why Was It Said?

What is the purpose in the passage? The Bible itself states purposes for some books and passages:

> **And many other signs truly did Jesus in the presence of His disciples, which are not written in this book:**
>
> **But these are written, that ye might believe that Jesus is the Christ, the Son of God; and that believing ye might have life through His name. (John 20:30-31)**

For other parts of Scripture the reason for writing is not so clearly stated. You must examine the context more closely to determine why the message was recorded.

5. When Was It Said?

The time and circumstances of some scriptures help us understand the meaning. For example, when there was confusion in church services at the church of Corinth Paul wrote a special passage of scripture. He told the women to keep silent in the Church. Did this mean women could not sing, pray, teach, or worship out loud in the Church?

To find the answer, we must examine when, why, and to whom this was said. In Jewish church services men were seated on one side of the building and women on the other. The Corinthian women were disrupting services by shouting questions to their husbands on the other side of the room. This was the occasion when Paul found it necessary to write:

> **Let your women keep silence in the churches; for it is not permitted unto them to speak; but they are commanded to be under obedience, as also saith the law. (I Corinthians 14:34)**

Interpreting a Scripture within its context helps explain the meaning of the passage. Taking a verse out of context can result in incorrect understanding. Often the context of a Scripture in the Bible gives the interpretation. A good example of this is the parable of the sower in Matthew 13:1-9. If you continue to read the context, the parable is interpreted in verses 18-23. In many cases similar to this the Bible interprets itself within the context. This is why contextual consideration is important.

THE RULE OF FIRST MENTION

The rule of first mention is as follows: The first time a word, phrase, object, or incident is mentioned in the Bible, it gives the key to its meaning anywhere else it occurs.

For example, in Genesis 3 there is the first mention of fig leaves. Here, Adam used fig leaves to try to cover his own sin and nakedness by his own efforts. Fig leaves speak of self-righteousness, rejection of God's remedy, and an attempt to justify ones self before God.

This is the meaning of fig leaves wherever they are mentioned afterwards in the Bible. For example, the last time fig leaves are mentioned is by Jesus in Matthew 21 and Mark 11 and 13. Here we find a fig tree with leaves but no fruit. Jesus cursed it and it withered away. To understand this act we need to remember the law of first mention and go back to Genesis 3. Fig leaves represent man's rejection of God's remedy and a self-righteous attempt to justify himself. The fig tree represented the self-righteous nation of Israel who had rejected Jesus. They rejected Him as King and would not accept His plan of salvation from sin. They were trying to be righteous through their own self-efforts.

THE RULE OF REPETITION

All the Bible is divinely inspired. There are no unessential parts of the Bible. Each word is inspired and necessary. For this reason, when something is repeated in Scripture it is for special emphasis. It means that a truth is of such special importance that it needs to be repeated.

John 3 illustrates this rule of repetition. Jesus tells Nicodemus of the necessity of the new birth experience and repeats it three times:

> **Except a man be born again, he cannot see the kingdom of God.**
> **(John 3:3)**

> **Except a man be born of water and of the Spirit he cannot enter into the kingdom of God. (John 3:5)**

> **Marvel not that I say unto thee, Ye must be born again. (John 3:7)**

Remember: Whenever the Bible repeats, it is the Holy Spirit's way of saying "Stop and really look at this."

THE RULE OF CUMULATIVE REVELATION

This rule is actually stated in the Bible:

Know this first, that no prophecy of the Scripture is of any private interpretation.

For the prophecy came not in old time by the will of men; but holy men of God spake as they were moved by the Holy Ghost. (II Peter 1:20- 21)

The Schofield Bible gives this translation:

No prophecy of scripture is its own interpretation; That is, it is not isolated from all the that the Word has given elsewhere.

The rule of cumulative revelation is this: The full truth of God's Word on any subject must not be gathered from an isolated passage. The cumulative (total) revelation of all the Bible says regarding a truth must be considered. This is why it is called the rule of "cumulative" revelation.

You cannot base your doctrine, teaching, or beliefs on a few isolated verses about a subject. You must keep studying until your interpretation becomes consistent with the whole of the Scriptures.

SELF-TEST

1. Write the Key Verse from memory.

_____

_____

_____

2. What does it mean to "rightly divide" the Word of truth?

_____

3. What is meant by "verbal" inspiration of the Bible?

_____

4. What is meant by "plenary" inspiration of the Bible?

_____

5. List each rule for interpretation which was discussed in this chapter. After each rule explain briefly what it means:

Rule 1:_____What it means:_____

Rule 2:_____What it means:_____

Rule 3:_____What it means:_____

Rule 4:_____What it means:_____

Rule 5:_____What it means:_____

Rule 6:_____What it means:_____

(Answers to tests are provided at the conclusion of the final chapter in this manual.)

FOR FURTHER STUDY

There are several passages in the Bible which confirm the inspiration of the Word by God. Look up each passage in your Bible and summarize it:

Scripture   **Summary**

Hebrews 1:1   _____
                                                   _____

I Thessalonians 2:13   _____
                                                   _____

II Timothy 3:16   _____
                                                   _____

I Corinthians 14:37   _____
                                                   _____

I Corinthians 2:7-13   _____
                                                   _____

I Corinthians 11:23   _____
                                                   _____

Galatians 1:11,12,16,20   _____
                                                   _____

Ephesians 3:1-10   _____
                                                   _____

I Peter 1:10,11,21   _____
                                                   _____

II Peter 3:16   _____
                                                   _____

CHAPTER SEVEN

BIBLE BACKGROUND

OBJECTIVES:

Upon completion of this chapter you will be able to:

- Write the Key Verse from memory.
- Identify major historical periods of the Bible.
- Describe everyday life in Bible times.
- Define Biblical archaeology.

KEY VERSE:

> **Concerning thy testimonies, I have known of old that thou hast founded them for ever. (Psalm 119:152)**

INTRODUCTION

Each part of the Bible occurred at a specific time in history and in a specific cultural context. Proper understanding of a passage often relates to these factors. This chapter gives a brief summary of the history of the Bible and explains details of everyday life in Bible days.

CHRONOLOGICAL HISTORY

Chronological history tells when an event occurred in the past. "Chronological" means in order or sequence. Chronological history organizes events of the past in proper order.

In most of the world the dating of time is divided into two major periods. These two periods are shown by the use of initials after the number of the year:

B.C. Numbers marked with these initials mean an event happened before the birth of Christ.

A.D. Numbers marked with these initials mean an event happened after the time of the birth of Christ.

When we say something happened 250 B.C., it means it happened 250 years Before Christ. When we say an event happened 700 A.D., it means it happened 700 years after the birth of Christ. When a number has B.C. after it, the larger the number is the older the date is. When a number has an A.D. after it, the larger number is the more recent date.

This chart will help you understand dating:

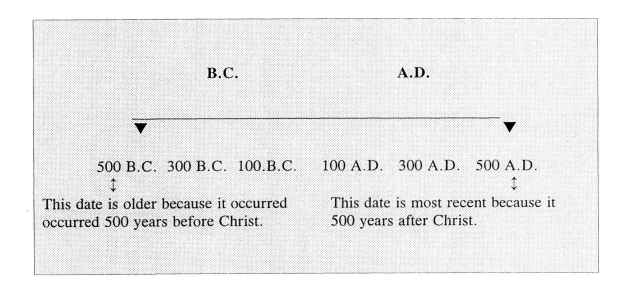

There are several ways we are able to know the chronological history of Bible events:

1. The Bible itself provides the dates of some events.

2. Early records of historians provide dates.

3. Through archaeology, which is the study of ancient things. It is a science which gains knowledge of times past from the study of existing remains of their civilizations. Biblical archaeology is the study of remains found in Bible lands. Some of the historical record of the Bible has been gained by dating these remains.

CHRONOLOGICAL HISTORY OF THE BIBLE

The chronological history of the Bible is most easily divided into twelve major periods. Chart One shows the major periods of Bible chronology. Look at Column Two on the chart. It shows the 12 periods of Bible history starting with "Creation to Abraham" and concluding with "Spread Of The Gospel."

Columns One and Three show when the books of the Bible were written. Note that between the Old and New Testament there was a period of 386 years during which no books were written. Refer to this chronology as you study the Bible. It will help you determine when events happened:

Chart One Chronological History Of The Bible

One	Two	Three
One	**Two**	**Three**
GENESIS	1. Creation to Abraham	
	2. Abraham to Moses	
EXODUS		
LEVITICUS	3. The Exodus	
NUMBERS		
DEUTERONOMY		
JOSHUA	4. The Conquest	
JUDGES	5. The Judges	
RUTH		
	6. The Kingdom	JOB
		PSALMS
		PROVERBS
		ECCLESIASTES
		SONG OF SOLOMON
I SAMUEL		ISAIAH
II SAMUEL		JEREMIAH
		LAMENTATIONS
I KINGS		EZEKIEL
II KINGS		DANIEL
		HOSEA
		JOEL
		AMOS
I CHRONICLES	7. Two kingdoms	OBADIAH
II CHRONICLES	8. Judah alone	JONAH
		MICAH
		NAHUM
		HABAKKUK
	9. The captivity	ZEPHANIAH
EZRA		
NEHEMIAH		HAGGAI
MALACHI	10. The Restoration	ZECHARIAH

(Chart One, Continued)

Between The Testaments

One	Two	Three
One	**Two**	**Three**
MATTHEW MARK LUKE JOHN	11. Life of Christ	
ACTS	12. Spread of the Gospel	ROMANS I AND II CORINTHIANS GALATIANS EPHESIANS PHILIPPIANS COLOSSIANS I AND II THESSALONIANS II AND II TIMOTHY PHILEMON TITUS HEBREWS JAMES I AND II PETER I , II, AND III JOHN JUDE REVELATION

Now read the description of major events which occurred in these 12 periods of Bible history:

1. <u>Creation to Abraham</u> (From creation to 2000 B.C.):

The creation of the universe, the fall of man into sin, the murder of Abel by Cain, Noah and the flood, and the Tower of Babel are some of the major Bible events of this period.

2. Abraham to Moses (200-1500 B.C.):

This period covers approximately 500 years. The experiences of one man, Abraham, and his descendants are the focus of this period. From Abraham God raised up the nation of Israel through which He wanted to reveal Himself to the nations of the world. This period includes the stories of Isaac, the son of Abraham, and of Isaac's son, Jacob. The period climaxes with the story of Joseph, Jacob's son, who was sold into slavery in Egypt and became a great ruler. Jacob and his family later joined Joseph in Egypt.

3. The Exodus (1500-1460 B.C.):

Between the close of Genesis and the opening of Exodus approximately 100 years passed. The family of Jacob multiplied into the nation of Israel during this time. The Egyptians became fearful because of the rapid increase of the Israelites so they made them slaves. Moses was raised up and under his leadership the Israelites miraculously departed from Egypt. After spending a year at Mt. Sinai, they wandered for 38 years in the desert. This period closes with the death of Moses and the leadership of Israel being assumed by a man named Joshua.

4. The Conquest of Canaan (1460-1450 B.C.):

During this period Joshua led Israel into Canaan to possess the land God had promised them. When the ungodly people of this area were conquered militarily, the land was divided among the 12 tribes of Israel. This period of 10 years is recorded in the book of Joshua.

5. The Judges (1450-1102 B.C.):

This was a time during which God raised up judges to rule the people of Israel. It is a dark period of time in the story of Israel as it was a time of spiritual failure. This period lasted for 348 years.

6. The Kingdom (1102-982 B.C.):

Samuel, the last judge of Israel, established the Kingdom of Israel and anointed Saul to be king. Three kings, Saul, David, and Solomon each reigned about 40 years. During this time the nation of Israel attained the highest glory in their history. The government was firmly established and Israel's borders were expanded. The story of this period, as well as the three following periods, are recorded in I and II Samuel, I and II Kings, and I and II Chronicles. The kingdom period lasted for 120 years and then the kingdom was divided.

7. The Two Kingdoms (982-722 B.C.):

When the evil son of Solomon, Rehoboam, came to the throne, the Northern tribes revolted. They established a separate kingdom of Israel. The Kingdom in the south became known as the Kingdom of Judah. For about 259 years Israel was divided into these two kingdoms.

8. Judah alone (722-587 B.C.):

Israel, the Northern Kingdom, was conquered by the Assyrians in 722 B.C. The people were taken captive into Assyria. After the fall of Israel, the southern Kingdom of Judah lasted 135 years. Judah's kings had shown more loyalty to God and the people had not gone so deep into sin.

9. The Captivity (587-538 B.C.):

In spite of the warnings of the prophets, Judah finally went deeper into sin until God let them be conquered by Nebuchadnezzar and taken captive into Babylon. The city of Jerusalem was destroyed and the people of God, who a few hundred years before had miraculous crossed the Jordan River, now marched away in chains.

10. The Restoration (538-391 B.C.):

When a king by the name of Cyrus became leader of Babylon, he permitted God's people to return and rebuild Jerusalem and their temple of worship. Zerubbabel led the group who returned to reestablish themselves in the promised land. The records of this period are found in the books of Ezra, Nehemiah, and Esther. This period of restoration lasted for 147 years.

Between the Testaments (391-5 B.C.)

The Old Testament closes with the reestablishment of God's people, Israel, in Canaan. Then came a period of about 400 years between the Old and New Testaments. There were no Bible books written during this period so information on the time comes from secular writings.

During this time Palestine was ruled by the Persians (536-333 B.C.), the Greeks (333-323 B.C.), the Egyptians (323-204 B.C.), the Syrians (204-165 B.C.), the Maccabeans (165-63 B.C.), and Rome (63 B.C. through the time of Christ).

11. Life of Christ (5 B.C. to 28 A.D.):

After 400 years, John the Baptist was raised up by God to prepare the way for the coming of Jesus Christ. Jesus was to be the Savior of sinful mankind. The promise of this plan of salvation was first made in the garden of Eden when man originally sinned (Genesis 3:15). Jesus was miraculously born of a virgin, revealed Himself to Israel as the Messiah, was rejected, crucified for the sins of all mankind, and resurrected by the power of God. Matthew, Mark, Luke and John record this period of 33 years.

12. The spread Of The Gospel (28-100 A.D.):

This period covers the events after Christ's return to Heaven following His resurrection. It records the spread of the Gospel from Jerusalem to Judea, Samaria, and throughout the world,

Chart Two: Judges Of Israel

The Old Testament refers to many events which happened when Israel was ruled by Judges. Judges ruled before Israel had kings. The stories of the judges are recorded in the book of Judges. Use this chart to help you identify when events occurred during the period of the judges:

Reference	Name	Dates B.C.	Number of Years
Judges 3:7-11	Othniel	1400-1360	40
Judges 3:12-31	Ehud	1360-1280	80
Judges 3:12-31	Shamgar	1280	1
Judges 4-5	Deborah	1280-1240	40
Judges 6-8:32	Gideon	1240 -1200	40
Judges 9	Abimelech	1200-1197	3
Judges 10:1-2	Tola	1197-1174	23
Judges 10:3-5	Jair	1174-1152	22
Judges 10:6-12	Jephthah	1152-1146	6
Judges 10:6-12	Ibzan	1146-1138	8
Judges 10:6-12	Elon	1138-1128	10
Judges 10:6-12	Abdon	1128-1121	7
Judges 13-16	Sampson	1121-1101	20

Chart Three: Kings Of Israel And Judah

Many Old Testament events are mentioned as having occurred during the reigns of different kings of Israel and Judah. This chart will help you date these events:

Kings Of Israel:

Name Of King	Length Of Reign In Years	Dates B.C.	Reference
Jeroboam I	22	976-954	I Kings 11:26-14:20
Nadab	2	954-953	I Kings 15:25-28
Baasha	24	953-930	I Kings 15:27-16:7
Elah	2	930-929	I Kings 16:6-14
Zimri	(7 days)	929	I Kings 16:9-20
Omri	12	929-918	I Kings 16:15-28
Ahab	21	918-898	I Kings 16:28-22:40
Ahaziah	1	898-897	I Kings 22:40-II Kings 1:18
Jehoram	11	897-885	II Kings 3:1-9:25
Jehu	28	885-857	II Kings 9:1-10:36
Jehoahaz	16	857-841	II Kings 13:1-9
Jehoash	16	841-825	II Kings 13:10-14:16
Jeroboam II	40	825-773	II Kings 14:23-29
Zechariah	½	773-772	II Kings 14:29-15:12
Shallum	(1 month)	772	II Kings 15:10-15
Menahem	10	772-762	II Kings 15:14-22
Pekahiah	2	762-760	II Kings 15:22-26
Pekah	20	760-730	II Kings 15:27-31
Hoshea	9	730-721	II Kings 15:30-17:6

Kings Of Judah:

Name Of King	Length Of Reign In Years	Dates B.C.	References
Rehoboam	17	976-959	I Kings 11:42-14:31
Abijam	3	959-996	I Kings 14:31-15:8
Asa	41	956-915	I Kings 15:8-24
Jehosphahat	25	915-893	I Kings 22:41-50
Johoram	8	893-886	II Kings 8:16-24
Ahaziah	1	886-885	II Kings 8:24-9:29
Athliah	6	885-879	II Kings 11:1-20
Joash	40	879-840	II Kings 11:1-12:21
Amaziah	29	840-811	II Kings 14:1-20
Azariah (Uzziah)	52	811-759	II Kings 15:1-7
Jotham	18	759-743	II Kings 15:32-38
Ahaz	19	743-727	II Kings 16:1-20
Hezekiah	29	727-698	II Kings 18:1-20:21
Manasseh	55	698-643	II Kings 21:1-18
Amon	2	643-640	II Kings 21:19-26
Josiah	31	640-609	II Kings 22:1-23:30
Jehohaz	(3 months)	609	II Kings 23:31-33
Jehoiakim	11	609-597	II Kings 23:34-24:5
Jehoiachin	(3 months)	597	II Kings 24:6-16
Zedekiah	11	597	II Kings 24:17-25:30

Chart Four: Old Testament Prophets

Since much of the Old Testament are books of prophecy, it is important to know when the prophets lived and prophesied. Use this chart to date events during the periods of the prophets.

Name Of Prophet	Prophesied To	Dates
Jonah	Assyria	Before Captivity (800-650)
Nahum	Assyria	Before Captivity (800-650)
Obadiah	Edom	Before Captivity (800)
Hosea	Israel	Before Captivity (750)
Amos	Israel	Before Captivity (750)
Isaiah/Jeremiah	Judah	Before Captivity (800-606)
Jeremiah/Lamentations	Judah	Before Captivity (800-606)
Joel	Judah	Before Captivity (800-606)
Micah	Judah	Before Captivity (800-606)
Habakkuk	Judah	Before Captivity (800-606)
Zephaniah	Judah	Before Captivity (800-606)
Ezekiel	Judah	During Captivity (606-536)
Daniel	Judah	During Captivity (606-536)
Haggai	Judah	After Captivity (536-400)
Zechariah	Judah	After Captivity (536-400)
Malachi	Judah	After Captivity (536-400)

LIFE IN BIBLE TIMES

The Bible, historians, and archaeological studies have provided information on the everyday life of the people of Israel in Bible times. Prior to the time when they went to Egypt the people of Israel lived in tents. They moved about with their flocks and herds in search of fresh pasture and water.

After the exodus from Egypt and the years traveling in the desert, Israel settled in their promised land of Canaan. From that time on the life of ordinary people followed a pattern that changed little throughout the years.

Peasant men worked either in the fields or in a village craft while the women and children kept the home. Farming and shepherding were both important occupations. There was some fishing and all kinds of village crafts including carpentry, pottery, and leather work.

Water was in short supply since the land was hot and dry most of the year. Water was drawn from a village well in a goatskin bucket. This was an important place of socializing for the women.

People wore long flowing robes in order to keep cool. The material of the robe was decided by wealth. The wealthy could afford brightly dyed cloth. Often clothes indicated a man's profession. For example, the priests wore special clothing and the rabbi (religious leader of Israel) wore a blue-fringed robe. Shoes were made of cow hide soles with leather thongs which fastened to the ankle.

Marriages were arranged by parents and there was little social mixing between young people. Because the bride was a working asset, she had to be paid for with a bride price. Domestic life centered in the home.

In Old Testament times there was no school for common men's children. They were taught skills and religion by their parents. By the time of Jesus, a girl's education was still entirely her mother's responsibility. Boys went to a school at the synagogue from age six on. The Old Testament was the textbook they used to learn history, geography, literature, and law. Exceptional students were sent to Jerusalem to learn from the Rabbis. Each boy also had to learn a trade. When a boy became 13 years old, he became "Bar Mitzvah" which is Jewish for "a son of the law." This meant that he was considered to be a man.

Death among the people of Israel called for elaborate ceremonies of mourning. Sometimes professional mourners would be hired. In New Testament times bodies were anointed and wrapped in special grave clothes. Poor people were buried in common graves or caves, but the wealthy had tombs dug out of rocks and sealed with a flat boulder.

There was no division between civil and religious law in Israel. The gate of the city or village was the place where problems were formally judged. The highest court in New Testament times was the Sanhedrin which consisted of 70 men who met in the temple. The Roman authorities, who were in control of Israel during New Testament times, allowed the Israelites to pass any sentence under their law except the death penalty.

The religious life of Israel centered first on the tabernacle and later on the temple in Jerusalem. Old Testament religious regulations were administered by the priests and the Levites. The greatest religious day of the year was the day of Atonement. On this day the high priest entered the innermost room of the temple to make atonement for his own sins and the sins of the people.

Other festivals included the Passover, which was a way of remembering Israel's escape from Egypt. The feast of Pentecost marked the beginning of harvest and the feast of Tabernacles was the harvest festival. The feast of Purim recalled Esther's deliverance of Israel, and the feast of trumpets marked the start of the new year.

Between the end of the Old Testament and the beginning of the New Testament regular worship shifted from the main temple to the local synagogue. This practice started in the days when Israel was in captivity and there was no temple in Jerusalem. Only men took an active part in the synagogue service. The women and children sat in a different section. The pattern of the service included statement of a creed, prayers, and readings from the law and prophets. This was followed by a sermon and a time when the men could question the minister.

The Old Testament Scriptures were written on sacred scrolls which only the doctors of law might open. Whenever possible visits were made to the temple at Jerusalem which had been rebuilt. The temple was similar to Solomon's original temple of Old Testament times but on a larger scale.

The story of the Bible is set against this background of traditional family and rural life which did not change for centuries. It was also set against the background of warring empires around Israel and the influence of the Roman Empire. Rome had extended to control the people of Israel during the time of Jesus.

SELF-TEST

1. Write the Key Verse from memory.

_____

_____

2. Matching: For each period in List One find the description that best fits it in List Two and write the letter on the blank in front of the period it describes.

List One: Periods

_____ Creation To Abraham
_____ Abraham to Moses
_____ The Exodus
_____ The Conquest
_____ The Judges

_____ The Kingdom
_____ The Two Kingdoms

_____ Judah Alone
_____ The Captivity
_____ The Restoration
_____ Life of Christ

_____ Spread of the Gospel

List Two

a. Acts and the Epistles tell this story.
b. Matthew, Mark, Luke, and John tell this story.
c. Israel's deliverance from Egypt happened.
d. Israel conquered the Promised Land during this period.
e. This was a period of great sin during which God raised up judges to deliver Israel.
f. Israel was split into two kingdoms in this period.
g. A period during which Saul, David, and Solomon reigned as kings.
h. Israel and Judah were in bondage during this period.
i. Jerusalem and the temple were rebuilt during this period.
j. Judah was the only kingdom.
k. The stories of Noah, Cain, Abel, and Tower of Babel happened during this period.
l. Abraham, Isaac, Jacob, and Joseph were key men during this period.

3. History or chronology tells _____ it happened.

4. What is Biblical archaeology?

_____

_____

_____

(Answers to tests are provided at the conclusion of the final chapter in this manual.)

FOR FURTHER STUDY

1. If you are especially interested in Bible chronology obtain the New Chronological Bible published by World Bible Publishers. The Chronological Bible is a King James version of the Bible which is organized on the basis of chronology. This means that instead of being organized by books (Genesis through Revelation) that the chapters and verses are presented in chronological order that events happened in the past or will occur in the future.

The content of Genesis through Revelation is organized in the Chronological Bible under twelve major sections:

-Development of the Early World
-Development of Israel As A Tribe
-Development of Israel As A Nation
-Development of Israel and As Kingdom
-Division of Israel into Dual Kingdoms
-Survival of Israel in the Southern Kingdom
-Captivity of Israel in Babylonia
-Restoration of Israel as a Nation
-Preservation of Israel during the Intertestamental period
  (this is the period of time between the writing of the Old and New Testaments)
-Inauguration of the Kingdom of God on Earth
-Continuation of the Kingdom of God on Earth
-Consummation of the Kingdom of God on Earth

The Narrated Bible published by Harvest House Publishers, Eugene, Oregon, is also a good tool for chronological study of the Bible. This book does not give the actual Bible text, but provides Bible references in chronological order and a brief narrative (commentary) on each reference.

2. If you are interested in Biblical archaeology, the following books are suggested:

Beginnings In Biblical Archaeology by Howard Vos published by Moody Press, Chicago, Illinois, U.S.A.

Archaeology in Bible Lands by Howard Vos published by Moody Press, Chicago, Illinois, U.S.A.

CHAPTER EIGHT

OUTLINING, MARKING, CHARTING

OBJECTIVES:

Upon completion of this chapter you will be able to:

- Write the Key Verse from memory.
- Use a method of Bible marking.
- Create an outline.
- Create a summarizing chart.

KEY VERSE:

> **The righteousness of thy testimonies is everlasting: give me understanding, and
> I shall live. (Psalm 119:144)**

INTRODUCTION

The development of three basic skills will improve any method of Bible study. These skills are marking, outlining, and charting. They are the subjects of this chapter.

MARKING

Marking is a method of emphasizing key Bible passages. Marking makes it easy for you to locate verses on specific subjects. To mark your Bible you underline selected verses. If you have different colors of pencils you can color code your underlining. If you do not have colored pencils you can use symbols in the margin by key verses.

Use the following colors or codes:

Red: For verses which relate to salvation. Red represents the blood of Jesus. You could also use the symbol of a cross for verses about salvation.

Green: This is the color of growing things. Use this color to underline verses about spiritual growth. You could also use a flower to represent growth.

Blue: This is the color of the heavens. Use this color to mark verses relating to the second coming of Jesus Christ, the New Jerusalem, and Heaven. If you are using symbols, use a crown to mark the verses in the margin of your Bible. The crown represents the Kingdom of Heaven.

Brown: A field of wheat ready to harvest is brown in color. Jesus used the example of harvest when speaking of evangelism. Use the color brown to mark verses related to evangelism. You could also use the symbol (#) which is a symbol standing for the word number. Use it to remind you of the great number of people who have yet to hear the Gospel message.

You can select additional colors to mark verses on other important subjects: Purple, pink, yellow, black, etc.

You can also use additional symbols and assign them meanings: ♡ ⌂ ✚ ♰ ★ ● ▲ ← ⊃

OUTLINING

An outline is a method of organizing study notes. It puts information in summary form to use in ministry and future study. An outline centers on a selected theme. This theme becomes the title of the outline which usually reflects the subject of study.

After identifying the subject of study, the next step is to identify main points which tell something about the subject. Next there will be sub-points. The prefix "sub" means they come under or tell something about the main point.

There are many ways to outline. We have selected one which uses special numbers called Roman numerals for the main points. If you are not familiar with Roman numerals, a list is provided for you in the "For Further Study" section of this chapter.

Subpoints on the outline are shown with capital letters of the alphabet. If there are further points under these, they are shown with regular numbers. Study the following example which summarizes how to make an outline:

PLACE THE TITLE HERE

I.   This is the Roman numeral for "1" used for the first main point.

     A.   This is a capital letter used for a subpoint relating to the main point.
          1.   If there was another subpoint relating to this, it would be marked with the number 1.
          2.   Perhaps there are other points relating back to subpoint A. If so, continue to place them in numerical order.

     B.   Main point I may have several subpoints. If so, continue down through the alphabet using capital letters in order. Each one of these subpoints should relate to the main point.

II.   To present another main point use the next Roman numeral.

     A.   Subpoints follow the same pattern under every main point.

As an example, we have prepared a brief outline of Romans 12:1-2. First read the verses:

I beseech you therefore, brethren, by the mercies of God, that ye present your bodies a living sacrifice, holy, acceptable unto God, which is your reasonable service.

And be not conformed to this world; but be ye transformed by the renewing of your mind, that ye may prove what is that good, and acceptable, and perfect will of God. (Romans 12:1-2)

The outline of this passages follows:

```
                    STEPS FOR FINDING GOD'S WILL

    I.      Present your bodies a living sacrifice:

            A.      Holy.
            B.      Acceptable unto God.

    II.     Be not conformed to this world:

            A.      Be transformed.
                    1.      We are transformed by the renewing of our minds.

    III.    These steps will help us prove (find) the will of God which is:

            A.      Good.
            B.      Acceptable.
            C.      Perfect.
```

You can see how this outline clearly summarizes the steps to God's will given in Romans 12:1-2.

CHARTING

Another method of organizing study materials is through charting. You will be given several charts to complete during this course to help you develop this skill. Charting is important because it helps you visualize what you have studied. Charting summarizes in brief form what you learn and helps you remember it.

There are two basic ways to draw a chart:

HORIZONTAL CHART:

Draw your chart lengthwise on a sheet of paper. Draw a line across the page and block off as many divisions as needed for your particular study. The horizontal chart is good to use in book study. You can find an example of it in Chapter Eleven.

VERTICAL CHART:

This type of chart is drawn vertically on a sheet of paper. A large rectangle is drawn and divisions are made within it. Vertical charts are best for shorter portions of material or for chapter studies.

Here is an example of a vertical chart on James 1:26-27.

First read the passage:

If any man among you seem to be religious, and bridleth not his tongue, but deceiveth his own heart, this man's religion is vain.

Pure religion and undefiled before God and the Father is this, To visit the fatherless and widows in their affliction, and to keep himself unspotted from the world. (James 1:26-27)

Now study the chart:

TESTS OF RELIGION

Personal Description	Test	Result	Religion
Seems to be religious	Control of tongue tongue	Deceives himself	Vain
Unspotted from world	Visits poor, Keeps self holy	Undefiled before God	Pure, undefiled

SELF-TEST

1. Write the Key Verse from memory.

_____

_____

2. What is wrong with the following outline structure?

_____

TITLE

I.   This is the first main point.

    A.   This is a subpoint relating to the main point.

    B.   This is the second main point.

3. What are the two main ways to draw charts?

_____

_____

4. What is meant by "marking" as related to Bible study?

_____

_____

_____

(Answers to tests are provided at the conclusion of the final chapter in this manual.)

FOR FURTHER STUDY

1. Study James 3:2-6 in your Bible. Complete the outline below:

THE HUMAN TONGUE

I.   If we offend not in word we are: (see verse 2)

    A.

    B.

II.   Examples of the power of small things:

    A.   The bit in a horse's mouth is used for two purposes: (see verse 3)

        1.

        2.

    B.   The helm of a ship: (verse 4)

        1.

    C.   A small fire: (verse 5)

        1.

III. The tongue is also small but it: (verses 5-6)

    A. Boasts great things.

    B. Is a world of iniquity.

    C.

    D.

    E.

2. Now complete the following chart which covers a portion of James 3:2-6:

THE TONGUE: A COMPARISON

Example	Result
Bit in horse's mouth	Turns their whole body
Helm in ship	
A small fire	
Human tongue	

3.   The following chart of Roman numerals is for use in creating outlines according to the pattern given in this chapter:

1	I	30	XXX
2	II	40	XL
3	III	50	L
4	IV	60	LX
5	V	70	LXX
6	VI	80	LXXX
7	VII	90	XC
8	VIII	100	C
9	IX		
10	X		
11	XI	Follow this same pattern (I, II, III) for each set.	
12	XII	For example, 32 would be XXXII	
13	XIII		
14	XIV		
15	XV		
16	XVI		
17	XVII		
18	XVIII		
19	XIX		
20	XX		

CHAPTER NINE

STUDYING THE BIBLE BY THE BIBLE

OBJECTIVES:

Upon completion of this chapter you will be able to:

- Write the Key Verse from memory.
- Identify symbols of the Word of God used in the Bible.
- Study God's Word by using the Bible.
- Identify the source of the Word.
- Distinguish between the milk and meat of the Word.

KEY VERSE:

Open thou mine eyes, that I may behold wondrous things out of thy law. (Psalm 119:18)

INTRODUCTION

One of the best ways to begin Bible study is to learn what the Bible says about itself. That is the subject of this chapter. In this lesson you will learn about the symbols of God's Word and specific facts about God's Word revealed in the Bible itself.

In most Institute courses when we refer to Scriptures we write them out within the context of the lesson. This is done to save you time. But we have not written out the verses in this lesson for a special reason. One of the purposes of this lesson is to familiarize you with using your Bible, so we have listed only the references. As you study the lesson, look up each reference in your Bible.

If you are not familiar with the location of the books, look in the front of your Bible. Most Bibles have a "Table Of Contents" which lists the page number where the book begins. When you find the page number listed for a book, you will be at chapter one of that book. Then look up the correct chapter and verse number:

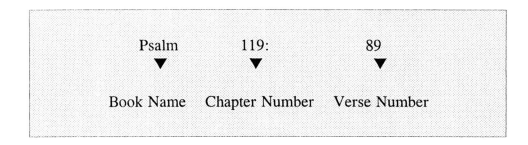

Psalm 119: 89

Book Name   Chapter Number   Verse Number

THE SOURCE OF THE WORD

The source of the Bible is God Himself. Read Psalm 68:11. This confirms that God is the source of the Word. I Thessalonians 2:13 explains that the Bible is God's Word and that its source is not man. When Jesus spoke during His earthly ministry, He made it clear that the source of His words was God. See John 14:10 and 24; 17:8 and 14; and 3:34.

THE HISTORY OF THE WORD

The Bible reveals much about its own history, answering questions such as "How long has the Word existed?" and "Who first wrote down the words of God?" Read Hebrews 11:3. This verse reveals that the world in which we live was framed (created) by the Word of God. Read Genesis chapter 1 in your Bible which tells the story of creation and you will find this to be true. God literally spoke the world into existence. You can read more about this in II Peter 3:5-7. Hebrews 1:3 says that He continues to uphold the world and all things by the Word of His power. Psalm 33:6 says that the heavens were made by the Word of God.

God is eternal. He has no beginning and end. Since God is inseparable from His Word (He is the Word), then the Word has no beginning and no end. Like God, His Word has always existed. Read Exodus 20:1-17 in your Bible. This is the first record of God inspiring a man (Moses) to write down His Words.

Read John chapter 1 in your Bible. Note closely verses 1-5 and 14. This passage refers to Jesus as the Word. It reveals that the Word (Jesus) was with God and was God in the beginning. It confirms how God and His Word created the world.

Jesus has always existed with the Father, but in verse 14 it tells how the Word (Jesus) became flesh and came to live on earth in human form. Verses 11-12 record how He was rejected by His own people but how those who receive Him can become children of God.

BOOKS, SCROLLS, AND STONES

God's Word was written in many forms throughout the years. It was written on stones by Moses

(Exodus 20:1-17) and on great stones when Israel entered the Promised Land (Deuteronomy 27:1-8).

God's Word was written in a book (Deuteronomy 31:24-26) and on scrolls (Jeremiah 36:2). A scroll is a long piece of paper with wooden spools (rollers) in each end. When you read or write on a scroll you start at one end and unroll the paper as you progress.

God even inspired songs in His Word. See Deuteronomy 31:19-22. David wrote God's Word in poetic form which was often sung. The book of Psalms is the worship and hymn book of the Bible.

INSPIRATION OF THE BIBLE

One of the most important things the Bible reveals about itself is that it is a book inspired by God. Through the inspiration of the Holy Spirit, God spoke to holy men to write His message.

Look up II Timothy 3:16-17 in your Bible. These verses confirm that God's Word is inspired. They also reveal that it is profitable in four major areas of Christian life:

-For doctrine
-For reproof
-For correction
-For instruction in righteousness

These verses are the main objectives of God's Word. These result in the man of God being perfect (mature) and thoroughly furnished (equipped) for all good works.

THE ETERNAL WORD

In the natural world many books are valid only for a short period of time. For example, a book on medical procedures may be valid for a few years. When better medicines or better methods of treatment are developed the book is no longer applicable.

God's Word is eternal and applicable in all times. It was relevant in the past, it is relevant in the present, and it will be relevant in the future (see Psalm 119:89).

Read I Peter 1:23. This verse reveals that God's Word not only abides forever, it also lives forever. God is and always has been. We serve a living God. God is inseparable from His Word. Because God lives, His Word lives and is relevant for all time.

Read Isaiah 40:8. This verse confirms that God's Word will stand (exist) forever. It will not perish like the things you see around you in the natural world.

TWO BASIC DIVISIONS

The Bible speaks of two basic divisions of God's Word. There is the milk of the Word and the meat of the Word. The milk of the Word is basic truth easily understood. The meat of the Word is the deeper teachings of God's Word which bring spiritual maturity. You can read about these in Hebrews 5:13-14 and I Peter 2:2.

PURPOSES OF THE WORD

God gave His Word to accomplish specific purposes. A purpose is a goal or objective. According to the Bible, some of these purposes are as follows:

-The Word produces faith in the Gospel: Acts 4:4
-It cleanses: John 15:3; Ephesians 5:26
-If you hear and believe, it brings eternal life: John 5:24
-It is the basis for eternal judgment: John 12:48
-Unclean spirits are cast out by the Word: Matthew 8:16; Luke 4:36
-Miraculous signs follow preaching of the Word convincing of the truth of the Gospel: Mark 16:20
-It gives assurance of salvation: I John 1:2-6
-You are born again by the Word: I Peter 1:23; Psalm 119:41
-The Word bears record of the truth of the Gospel: I John 5:7
-You are sanctified by the Word: I Timothy 4:5
-There is hope in His Word: Psalm 130:5; 119:49, 81
-There is healing in His Word: Psalm 107:20
-It keeps you from the path of the destroyer: Psalm 17:4
-It is spirit and life: John 6:63
-It brings joy and rejoicing: Jeremiah 15:16
-Faith is increased by the Word: Romans 10:17
-It brings comfort: I Thessalonians 4:18: Psalm 119:50, 52
-It brings spiritual nourishment: I Timothy 4:6
-It brings answered prayer: John 15:7
-It is the key to success: Joshua 1:8
-If you hear and keep it you are blessed: Luke 11:28
-It is profitable for spiritual growth: II Timothy 3:16-17
-It brings blessings when it is kept and cursings when it is not kept: Deuteronomy 28
-It is a weapon in the time of temptation: Matthew 4
-It converts the soul: Psalm 19:7
-It makes wise the simple: Psalm 19:7
-It enlightens: Psalm 19:8
-It warns: Psalm 19:11
-Keeping the Word brings great reward: Psalm 19:11
-It permits access to Heaven: Revelation 22:14
-It brings the blessing of walking in righteousness: Psalm 119:1-3

-It makes you wiser than your enemies, teachers, and the ancients: Psalm 119:98-104
-It quickens: Psalm 119:25
-It strengthens: Psalm 119:28
-It is the basis of God's mercy towards you: Psalm 119:58
-It brings delight: Psalm 119:92
-It gives the simple understanding: Psalm 119:130, 169; 104
-It brings deliverance: Psalm 119:170

THE WORD IS NOT VOID

As we have seen, there are many purposes for God's Word. The Bible teaches that the Word will accomplish the purposes for which it exists. Read Isaiah 55:11. Here God says that His Word will not return void which means that God does not make empty promises. What He says will happen. Every word of the Bible was written for a purpose and that purpose will be accomplished.

SYMBOLS OF THE WORD

The Bible uses many different symbols to describe the Word of God. A symbol is something that represents something else. For example, each star in the flag of the United States of America represents one of the 50 states which make up that nation. The star is a symbol of a state. The following are symbols used in the Bible to describe God's Word. Look up each verse and read it in your Bible:

A Mirror: **James 1:23-27**

When you look into a mirror in the natural world, it reflects your physical image. When you look into God's Word, just like a mirror, the Bible reflects your true spiritual condition.

A Laver: **Ephesians 5:26-27**

A laver is the Biblical term for a basin which holds water used for cleansing. The water of the Word of God cleanses you spiritually.

A Lamp: **Psalm 119:105**
A Light: **Psalm 119:105,130; Proverbs 6:23**

Both a lamp and light give guidance. They enable you to see in the dark. The Word of God provides spiritual guidance and helps you find your way out of the darkness of sin.

Rain: **Isaiah 55:10-11**
Water: **Ephesians 5:26**

Both rain and water are refreshing. The Word of God is compared to rain and water because it refreshes you spiritually.

Food: **Jeremiah 15:16; I Peter 2:1-2; I Corinthians 3:1-2; Hebrews 5:12-14**
A Diet: **Hebrews 5:12**

The Bible is compared to food which quenches natural hunger because it quenches spiritual hunger. Just as food permits natural growth, the Bible permits spiritual growth. Some parts of the Bible are called the milk of the Word because they are easily understood. Other portions are called the meat of the Word because the passages are more difficult to understand. God wants you to progress from the milk to the meat of His Word. Learning how to study the Bible will help you accomplish this objective.

A Fire: **Jeremiah 23:29; 20:9**

In the natural world a fire is used to refine precious metals. The fire burns out all the impurities. God's Word acts as a fire in your spiritual life to burn out impure thoughts, words, and deeds.

A Hammer: **Jeremiah 23:29**

A hammer can break rock in pieces. The Word of God can take sin-hardened hearts, break them, and make them pliable in the hands of God.

A Scalpel: **Hebrews 4:12**

A scalpel is a sharp knife used by doctors for surgery to cure illness. God's Word performs spiritual surgery. It corrects spiritual sickness. It removes spiritual growths and infections from your life.

A Sword: **Ephesians 6:17**

A sword in the natural world is a weapon. The Word of God is your spiritual sword. It is a weapon to use against your spiritual enemy, Satan.

Medicine: **Psalm 119:25**

Just as medicine in the natural world cures physical illness, God's Word works as a medicine to cure spiritual sickness.

Seed: Matthew 13:1-23; Mark 4:1-20; Luke 8:4-15; I Peter 1:23; James 1:18

God's Word is like seed. When it is planted in your heart--if it finds receptive ground--it will grow and produce spiritual fruit in your life.

Honey: **Psalm 19:10**

Honey is a very sweet substance in the natural world. God's Word is compared to honey because it is sweet spiritually. Studying God's Word brings spiritual sweetness in your life.

Gold: **Psalm 19:9-10**

In the natural world, gold is one of the most precious metals. The Bible is compared to gold because of its spiritual value.

DESCRIPTION OF THE WORD

In addition to these symbols, the Bible provides other descriptions of God's Word. It is:

-The Spirit of Life: John 6:63
-The words of eternal life: John 6:68
-Precious: I Samuel 3:1
-Pure: Proverbs 30:5; Psalm 12:6; 19:7; 119:140
-Truth and soberness: Acts 26:25
-Truth: John 17:17; Colossians 1:5; Psalm 119:142
-True from the beginning: Psalm 119:160
-Tried: Psalm 18:3
-Right: Psalm 33:4; 19:8; 119:75
-The Word of life: I John 1:1; Philippians 2:6
-The Word of salvation: Acts 13:26
-The Word of faith: Romans 10:8
-Perfect: Psalm 19:7
-Counselor: Psalm 119:24
-Faithful: Psalm 119:86
-Settled: Psalm 119:89
-Heritage: Psalm 119:111
-Word of righteousness: Psalm 119:123
-Righteous and very faithful: Psalm 119:138
-Upright: Psalm 119:137
-Delight: Psalm 119:143

RESPONSE TO THE WORD

It is not enough to hear, read, or study God's Word. The Bible teaches that you must respond to God's Word. You are to:

-Let it fall upon good ground in your heart: Mark 4, Luke 8, Matthew 13
-Hear it and do it to be wise: John 12:47
-Keep the Word: John 14:23
-Believe on Jesus in order for God's Word to abide in you: John 5:38
-Continue in His Word: John 8:31
-Not live only on physical food, but also for the Word: Matthew 4:4; Luke 4:4; Deuteronomy 8:3
-Praise His Word: Psalm 56:4, 10
-Give thanks for it: Psalm 119:62
-Magnify His Word even above His name: Psalm 138:2
-Engraft His Word in your heart: James 1:21
-Be a doer of the Word and not a hearer only: James 1:22-23
-Ask forgiveness for sin so His Word can abide in you: I John 1:10
-Desire the milk of His Word: I Peter 2:2
-Let the Word of God dwell in you richly: Colossians 3:16
-Rightly divide the Word of God: II Timothy 2:5
-Search the Scriptures: John 5:39; Acts 17:11
-Declare His Word: Psalm 119:26-27
-Choose His Word: Psalm 119:30
-Stick to His Word: Psalm 119:31
-Run the way of His Word: Psalm 119:32
-Keep it: Psalm 119:33
-Observe it: Psalm 119:34
-Delight in it: Psalm 119:35; 70; 77; 143; 174
-Incline your heart unto it: Psalm 119:36
-Desire to have it established in your life: Psalm 119:38
-Long after it: Psalm 119:40
-Use it to answer others: Psalm 119:42
-Hope in it: Psalm 119:43, 47
-Keep it forever: Psalm 119:44
-Seek His precepts: Psalm 119:45
-Be willing to speak it before leaders: Psalm 119:46
-Meditate on it: Psalm 119:48; 78; 148
-Not decline from it: Psalm 119:52
-Walk according to its teachings: Psalm 119:59
-Not delay to keep His Word: Psalm 119:60
-Not forget it: Psalm 119:61, 83, 93, 153, 176
-Choose companions who also fear the Word and keep it: Psalm 119:63

-Believe it: Psalm 119:66; 128
-Keep it with your whole heart: Psalm 119:69
-Value it more than gold and silver: Psalm 119:72
-Desire to learn it: Psalm 119:73
-Hope in the Word: Psalm 119:74; 81
-Find comfort in it: Psalm 119:76;82
-Desire for it to change your heart: Psalm 119:80
-Not forsake it: Psalm 119:87
-Seek after it: Psalm 119:94
-Consider it: Psalm 119:95
-Long for God's Word: Psalm 119:131
-Order your steps in the Word: Psalm 119:133
-Be grieved when God's Word is not honored: Psalm 119:136; 158
-Stand in awe of God's Word: Psalm 119:161
-Love it: Psalm 119:163, 165, 167
-Speak His Word: Psalm 119:172

RESPONSIBILITY FOR THE WORD

In addition to making the proper response to God's Word, you have a responsibility for the Word of God. The early Church assumed this responsibility as they went everywhere preaching the Word of God (Acts 8;4; 13:49; 12:24). They asked God for boldness to speak the Word (Acts 4:29 and 31) and the Word of God increased throughout the world because of their efforts (Acts 6:7; 19:20)

Here is what the Bible reveals about YOUR responsibility for the Word of God:

-You are to preach His Word throughout the world: Matthew 16:15; Luke 24:47; Mark 16:15.
-If you are taught in God's Word then you have a responsibility to teach others: Galatians 6:6.
-You are to preach the Word: II Timothy 4:2
-You are to speak His Word without fear: Philippians 1:4.
-God puts His Word in you so you can speak it to others: Deuteronomy 18:18-19; Isaiah 51:16;
 Jeremiah 1:9; 3:12; 5:14; 26:12; Ezekiel 2:6-7.
-You should not speak your own words but you should speak His words: Isaiah 58:13
-You are not to be ashamed of the Word: Mark 8:38
-You are to teach it to your children: Deuteronomy 6:6-9

WARNINGS IN THE WORD

Here are some warnings God gives concerning His Word:

-Persecution comes because the Word of God is preached: Mark 4:7
-Some people will even be killed because of their witness for the Word: Revelation 6:9; 20:4.

-The Word can be ineffective in your life because of traditions of man: Mark 7:13.
-You can pervert the Word of the Lord: Jeremiah 23:36.
-You can corrupt the Word of the Lord: II Corinthians 2:17
-You can use the Word deceitfully: II Corinthians 4:2

The Bible says not to listen to every word you hear: Proverbs 14:15. (This means that every one who claims to speak God's Word is not really doing so.) There are false teachers who do not teach the true Word of God (Jude 1). You are to withdraw yourself from these people (I Timothy 6:3-5. False teachers do not speak the true Word of God. They speak their own words. They also speak:

Lying words:	Jeremiah 29:23
Vain words:	Ephesians 5:6
Enticing words:	Colossians 2:4
Flattering words:	I Thessalonians 2:5
Vain babblings:	I Timothy 6:21
Feigned words:	II Peter 2:3
Swelling words:	II Peter 2:18; Jude 16
Malicious words:	III John 10

In conclusion, the Bible gives a final warning regarding the Word in Revelation 22:18-19:

For I testify unto every man that heareth the words of the prophecy of this book, If any man shall add unto these things, God shall add unto him the plagues that are written in this book.

And if any man shall take away from the words the book of this prophecy, God shall take away his part out of the book of life, and out of the holy city and from the things which are written in this book. (Revelation 22:18-19)

SELF-TEST

1. Write the Key Verse from memory.

_____

_____

2. List at least five symbols used in the Bible to represent the Word of God.

_____

_____

_____

_____

3. Many purposes for the Word of God were listed in this chapter. Can you list at least three of them?

_____

_____

_____

4. Why are you not to believe every word you hear?

_____

5. What warning is given to those who add to God's Word?

_____

6. What warning is given to those who take away from what is written in God's Word?

_____

7. Who is the source of the Word?_____

8. Whose words did Jesus speak?_____

9. The two main divisions of Bible content are the_____and the_____of the Word.

10. According to the Biblical record, who was the first man to write down God's Words?

_____

(Answers to tests are provided at the conclusion of the final chapter in this manual.)

FOR FURTHER STUDY

Of all the chapters in the Bible, Psalm 119 speaks most frequently about the Word of God. It is also the longest chapter in the Bible.

There are several different words used to refer to God's Word in this chapter. Each time they are used they add to our knowledge of His Word. Read Psalm 119 and underline the following words each time they occur:

-word
-words
-judgments
-statutes
-precepts
-law
-commandments
-thy way
-thy testimonies

After you underline each use of these words in Psalm 119, read the chapter once again and create a chart to summarize your study. Follow the pattern below. List each verse number that contains one or more of these words and then summarize what the verse teaches about God's Word.

Continue this pattern:

Verse Number   **Summary**

1   We are blessed if we walk in His law.

_____
_____
_____
_____
_____
_____
_____
_____
_____

CHAPTER TEN

DEVOTIONAL BIBLE STUDY

OBJECTIVES:

Upon completion of this chapter you will be able to:

- Write the Key Verse from memory.
- List the steps of the devotional method of Bible study.
- Do a devotional Bible study.

KEY VERSE:

Mine eyes prevent the night watches, that I might meditate in thy word. (Psalm 119:148)

INTRODUCTION

The first method of Bible study which you will learn is called the devotional method. This chapter defines, explains, and presents an example of a devotional Bible study. The "For Further Study" section provides an opportunity to apply what you have learned by actually doing a devotional study.

THE METHOD DEFINED

The devotional method gets its name from the word "devotion" which means "dedication, consecration, worship, and sincere attachment to a cause or person." The devotional method of Bible study increases dedication and consecration to God. It leads to worship and a deeper personal relationship with the Lord Jesus Christ.

This method involves not only study of God's Word but also the application of its truths. It is against this method that Satan raises his greatest opposition. Satan is not concerned about study just to gain knowledge. He is vitally concerned when Bible study results in application which brings positive changes in your spiritual life. It is not enough to just be "hearers of the Word." A person who is a hearer of the Word is one who studies God's Word but never applies the Word to his life:

But be ye doers of the Word, and not hearers only, deceiving your own selves.

For if any be a hearer of the Word, and not a doer, he is like unto a man beholding his natural face in a glass;

For he beholdeth himself, and goeth his way, and straightway forgetteth what manner of man he was.

But whoso looketh into the perfect law of liberty, and continueth therein, he being not a forgetful hearer, but a doer of the work, this man shall be blessed in his deed. (James 1:22-25)

You will learn many methods of Bible study in this course but each method should result in application. Whether you do a book, chapter, verse, word, or any other study, you should always apply what you learn to your life and ministry.

THE METHOD EXPLAINED

Use the form provided in the "For Further Study" section of this lesson to do your devotional study. Here are the steps for doing the study:

STEP ONE: RECORD PASSAGE INFORMATION

Record the name of the book in which the passage you are studying is found. Then record the chapter and verse numbers you have selected to study.

STEP TWO: IDENTIFY THE SUBJECT

Read the portion of Scripture which you have selected to study. Select a title that summarizes the subject and record it on your chart.

STEP THREE: IDENTIFY THE KEY VERSE

Which verse provides the best summary of the Scripture portion you are studying? Write the verse and reference on your chart.

STEP FOUR: SUMMARIZE

In your own words, summarize what the portion of Scriptures teaches.

1. Outline the main points covered.

2. Use a chart to summarize the passage.

3. Make a brief summary statement.

4. Paraphrase the passage. Paraphrasing is when you take a verse and summarize it in your own words. Follow the text, but put it in the language of today. (See the example section of this chapter).

STEP FIVE: MEDITATE

It is important to read and study the Bible but you must also learn to meditate on God's Word. The word "meditate" means to think, dwell on, and ponder. After you select a Bible portion to study, identify its subject and key verse, and summarize its teachings, then meditate on the passage.

God told Joshua that meditating on His Word was the key to success:

> **This book of the law shall not depart out of thy mouth; but thou shalt meditate therein day and night, that thou mayest observe to do according to all that is written therein: for then thou shalt make thy way prosperous, and then thou shalt have good success. (Joshua 1:8)**

Read slowly through the passage. Read it aloud. Imagine the Lord speaking to you personally with this passage. Consider what it says to you personally by using some of the questions suggested under Step Six in this lesson.

One important way to meditate on the Word is to memorize it. When you memorize portions you are able to recall them at any time and think about them. The key verse you select is a good portion to memorize. Make some note cards as illustrated below. Write the verse on one side of the card. Write the reference where the verse is found on the other side of the card:

Side One:

Thy word have I hid in mine heart, that I might not sin against thee.

Side Two:

Psalm 119:11

Read the verse several times aloud and then try to repeat it without looking at the card. After you say the verse check your card to see if you have said it correctly. Look at the reference side of the card and try to say the verse. Look at the verse side of the card and try to remember the reference. Save your Scripture memory cards and continue to review and meditate on them.

STEP SIX: MAKE APPLICATION

Now you are ready to apply what you have learned during meditation. Application is when you personally apply to your life and ministry the truths you have learned. Sometimes you cannot immediately apply everything you learn, but begin to apply all you can. God will help you apply the truth of His Word even if it means you must take one small step at a time in the process of application.

The following questions will help you apply God's Word to your life:

Example to follow:

Is there an example to follow in this portion of Scripture?

Error to avoid:

Is there an error or sin which should be avoided?

Duty to perform:

Does this portion of Scripture call for action. Are you told to do something? If so, what action are you to take?

Promise to claim:

Is there a promise in this passage which you can claim?

Relationship to develop:

What does this passage teach about your relationship with God through Jesus Christ? What does it teach about God the Father, Jesus Christ the Son, and the Holy Spirit? What does it teach about your relationship with others in your family, community, church congregation, and the world. What does it teach about your relationship with yourself?

Changes to make:

What changes should you make in your life in view of what you have learned in this Scripture portion? Be specific.

Prayer to pray:

Pray a personal prayer regarding this passage. Ask God to help you apply the truths you have learned. Prayer personalizes the principles taught in God's Word. You may even want to write out your prayer as in the example provided in this chapter.

EXAMPLE OF THE DEVOTIONAL METHOD

STEP ONE: RECORD PASSAGE INFORMATION

Book: Galatians
Chapter: 5
Verses: 16-25

STEP TWO: IDENTIFY THE SUBJECT

Subject: Works of the Flesh and Fruit of the Spirit

STEP THREE: IDENTIFY THE KEY VERSE

Key Verse: If we live in the Spirit, let us also walk in the Spirit. (Galatians 5:25)

STEP FOUR: SUMMARIZE

1.   The following is an example of an **outline** summary:

WORKS OF THE FLESH AND FRUIT OF THE SPIRIT

I.   The flesh lusts against the Spirit and the Spirit against the flesh. Those who live in the flesh will not inherit the Kingdom of God. Fleshly works include:

    A.   Adultery
    B.   Fornication
    C.   Uncleanness
    D.   Lasciviousness
    E.   Idolatry
    F.   Witchcraft
    G.   Hatred
    H.   Variance
    I.   Emulations
    J.   Wrath
    K.   Strife
    L.   Seditions

113

M. Heresies
N. Envyings
O. Murders
P. Drunkenness
Q. Revellings

II. The fruit of the Holy Spirit which God desires to give us contrasts the works of the flesh:

A. Love
B. Joy
C. Peace
D. Longsuffering
E. Gentleness
F. Goodness
G. Faith
H. Meekness
I. Temperance

III. We are to:

A. Walk in the spirit (verse 16,25)
B. Be led of the spirit (verse 18)
C. Live in the spirit (verse 25)

2. The following is an example of a **summarizing chart**:

WORKS OF THE FLESH AND FRUIT OF THE SPIRIT
Galatians 5:16-25

Works of the Flesh (Fulfilling Lusts)	Fruit of the Spirit (Living in the Spirit)
Adultery	Love
Fornication	Joy
Uncleanness	Peace
Lasciviousness	Longsuffering
Idolatry	Gentleness
Witchcraft	Goodness
Hatred	Faith
Variance	Meekness
Emulations	Temperance
Wrath	
Strife	
Seditions	
Heresies	
Envyings	
Murders	
Drunkenness	
Revellings	

3. Here is an example of a **summary statement**:

This passage presents two contrasts: The lusts of the flesh and the fruit of the Holy Spirit. If we belong to Jesus, we are to crucify the lusts of the flesh and live, walk, and be led by the Holy Spirit. The works of the flesh are adultery, fornication, uncleanness, lasciviousness, idolatry, witchcraft, hatred, variance, emulations, wrath, strife, seditions, heresies, envyings, murders, drunkenness, revellings. The fruit of the Spirit is love, joy , peace, longsuffering, gentleness, goodness, faith, meekness, temperance.

4. Here is an example of a **paraphrase** of Galatians 5:24-25:

"Those who belong to Christ have destroyed the desires, loves, and lusts of the flesh. If we claim that the Holy Spirit lives in us, then we should act like it!"

STEP FIVE: MEDITATE

Verses to memorize and meditate on: Verses 16-18 and 25-26. Also memorize the list of spiritual fruit which God wants to develop in my life. Meditate and study on the meaning of each fruit of the Holy Spirit. What does it mean to be gentle, good, meek, temperate, etc?

STEP SIX: MAKE APPLICATION

Example to follow: Developing the fruit of the Holy Spirit in my life.

Error to avoid: Works of the flesh.

Duty to perform:

Walk in the Spirit	(verses 16,25)
Be led of the Spirit	(verse 18)
Live in the Spirit	(verse 25)

Promise to claim: "This I say then, Walk in the Spirit and ye shall not fulfill the lust of the flesh." Verse 16.

Relationships to develop: My relationships with others should demonstrate love, longsuffering, gentleness, meekness. I need to develop joy, peace, goodness, faith, and temperance in every area of my life. I learned that God wants my relationship to Him to be based on holiness in conduct. If I truly belong to Christ it will affect my relationship to others, myself, and God.

Changes to make: The three areas I need most to change:

Temperance:	Control my appetite. Develop self control and discipline.
Faith:	Be more believing of God's promises.
Love:	Show love to those around me who are unlovable.

Prayer to pray:

Dear Heavenly Father:

Help me walk in your Spirit, be led of your Spirit, and live each moment in your Spirit. Cleanse my life from the works of the flesh. Help me to crucify worldly desires. Develop the beautiful fruit of the Holy Spirit in me.

In Jesus name, amen.

SELF-TEST

1. Write the Key Verse from memory.

_____

_____

_____

2. What is the devotional method of Bible study?

_____

_____

3. List the six steps of the devotional method.

_____

_____

_____

_____

_____

_____

4. What does it mean to be a "doer of the Word" and not a "hearer" only? Give a Scripture reference to support your answer.

_____

5. Why does Satan fight the use of the devotional method of Bible study?

_____

(Answers to tests are provided at the conclusion of the final chapter in this manual.)

FOR FURTHER STUDY

Study Philippians 4:4-9 using the devotional method of Bible study. Use this form to do this and other devotional Bible studies.

DEVOTIONAL BIBLE STUDY

Book: **Chapter:**   **Verses:**   **Subject:**

Key Verse:

Summary:

Meditation:

Application:

Example to follow:

Error to avoid:

Duty to perform:

Promise to claim:

Relationship to develop:

Changes to make:

Prayer to pray:

CHAPTER ELEVEN

BOOK STUDY

OBJECTIVES:

Upon completion of this chapter you will be able to:

- Write the Key Verse from memory.
- Explain how to do a Bible book study.
- Do a Bible book study.
- Create a book study chart.
- Create an outline of a book of the Bible.

KEY VERSE:

Wherewithal shall a young man cleanse his way? by taking heed thereto according to thy Word. (Psalm 119:9)

INTRODUCTION

In this chapter you will learn how to survey an entire book of the Bible. You will also learn how to create a chart and an outline to summarize your studies. An example of the book study method is included and you are given the opportunity to do such a study in the "For Further Study" section of this chapter. In following chapters you will learn how to study the chapters, paragraphs, verses, and words of a book.

A book survey is an example of "synthetic" Bible study. This word means to study something as a whole to gain a general knowledge of its content. Later, when we divide a book into chapters, paragraphs, verses, and words, we will be doing "analytical" Bible study. To analyze something is to separate it into its various parts and examine each individually. An analytical study is more detailed than a synthetic study.

DEFINITION OF THE METHOD

A book study is important because the chapters, paragraphs, verses, and words of a book must be interpreted in proper context. A book study provides knowledge of this context.

EXPLANATION OF THE METHOD

Here are three steps to study a book of the Bible:

STEP ONE: INITIAL SURVEY:

Read the entire book at one sitting to identify the theme (subject) of the book. Choose a title that summarizes the theme. You will use this title on the Book Study Chart. This will also become the title of your outline.

Determine the purpose for which the book was written, to whom it was written, and the author. Some books state the name of the author but for the names of others you will need to consult an outside Bible study resource.*   Each author had a special reason for writing under the inspiration of the Holy Spirit. This purpose is usually reflected in the content of the book.

Determine the geographic setting of the book. This is where the events occurred. Record this on the Book Study Chart.

Summarize the basic life and ministry principle in one sentence. This is the basic truth of the book which is applicable to your life or ministry. There are many principles taught in a single book, but try to determine the most important for this summary statement.

Remember, the chapter divisions in the Bible are not divinely inspired. They were made by man for ease in locating specific passages in the Bible. When you read the entire book without chapter divisions you are reviewing the message as it was originally given.

In this first reading do not be concerned with details. Survey the book for general information: Theme, author, purpose, to whom, geographic setting, and basic life and ministry principle. Read quickly to gain an overview of the entire book. Do not stop and analyze what you are reading. You will do that later.

---

* If you do not have access to Bible study materials, this information is given in the Harvestime International Institute course entitled *"Basic Bible Survey."*

STEP TWO: BOOK STUDY CHART:

Read the book a second time. Note the major divisions of the book. These divisions may be determined by subject matter, events, biographical material, geographical settings, or other such factors.

Create titles for each chapter of the book. The chapter title should reflect the general content of a chapter but it should not be so general that it could fit any chapter of the Bible.   Think of titles as handles with which to grasp the content of the chapter. Keep them short so they are easy to remember. Enter these chapter titles on the Book Study Chart.

Select the key verse of the book. The key verse should be one that best summarizes the purpose or content of the book. Enter the reference on the Book Study Chart.

As you read, list the names of major characters in the space provided on the chart. This list will provide a selection from which to do biographical studies. You will learn how to do such studies later in this course.

Record key words and phrases on the chart. Key words and phrases are those basic to understanding the book.   They are often repeated frequently or explained in detail in the book. You can use this list for word studies which you will learn how to do later in this course.

STEP THREE: BOOK OUTLINE:

The final step in book study is to create an outline. Read the book again. As you read, create an outline of the entire book. Some of the division and chapter titles on your Book Study Chart will become main points in your outline.   The purpose of your outline is to summarize the entire content of the book.

EXAMPLE OF THE METHOD

STEP ONE: INITIAL SURVEY:

Book: The book selected for survey is Philippians.

Theme: The theme of the book is an appeal for Christian unity.

Author: The author of the book is the Apostle Paul.

Written To: The book was written to the Christians in the city of Philippi.

Purpose: The general purpose of the book was twofold: It was to thank the Philippians for their support of his ministry and appeal for Christian unity.

Key Words: Rejoice, joy.

Key Verse: Philippians 2:2

Characters: Euodias, Syntyce, Timotheus, Epaphroditus, Clement, Caesar's household.

Life And Ministry Principle: The basic life and ministry principle is unity brings joy.

STEP TWO: BOOK STUDY CHART:

Author:	Paul
To:	Believers at Philippi
Purpose:	To thank them for support and appeal for Christian unity
Key Words:	Rejoice, joy
Key Verse:	Philippians 2:2
Characters:	Euodias, Syntyce, Timotheus, Clement Epaphroditus, Caesar's household
Life And Ministry Principle:	Christian unity brings joy.

BOOK STUDY CHART
Name Of Book: Philippians
Title For Chart: An Appeal For Christian Unity

1	2	3	4	5

Chapter Titles

STEP THREE: BOOK OUTLINE:

Philippians: An Appeal For Christian Unity

I.   Introduction:
    A.   Greeting 1:1-2
        1.   From Paul and Timotheus.
        2.   To: Saints in Christ Jesus, bishops, and deacons at Philippi.
    B.   Prayer for Philippians 1:3-11
    C.   Personal matters 1:12-26
        1.   Events which have served to spread the Gospel 1:12-18
        2.   Faith that he will be released 1:19-21
        3.   His questioning as to whether it is best to live or die 1:22-26

II.   Exhortations for unity 1:27-2:18
    A.   Appeal for unity in suffering 1:27-30
    B.   Unity in Christ 2:1-11
    C.   Spiritual growth brings unity 2:12-18

III. Paul's plans 2:19-30
    A.   Hopes to send Timothy 2:19-23
    B.   Hopes to come himself 2:24
    C.   Is sending Epaproditus 2:25-30

IV.   Warnings 3:1-4:1
    A.   Against Judaizing teachers 3:1-16
    B.   Against false teachers 3:17-21

V.   Exhortations 4:1-9
    A.   Unity between Euodias and Syntyce 4:1-3
    B.   Unity in joy 4:4
    C.   Unity in moderation 4:5
    D.   Unity in prayer 4:6
    E.   Unity in mind 4:7-8
    F.   Unity between knowledge and actions 4:9

VI.   Thanks for their gift 4:10-20

VII. Benediction 4:21-23

SELF-TEST

1. Write the Key Verse from memory.

_____

_____

2. Write the number of the definition in front of the type of study it best describes.

Type Of Study   **Definition**

____Analytical Bible Study   1. To survey something for general content; a book survey.

____Synthetic Bible Study   2. To study the individual parts in detail.

3. List the three steps of the Book Study Method.

_____

_____

_____

4. What are six basic things to record when doing the initial survey of a book?

_____

_____

_____

_____

_____

_____

(Answers to tests are provided at the conclusion of the final chapter in this manual.)

FOR FURTHER STUDY

Do a book study of one of the New Testament books. For your first study we suggest that you choose one of the shorter books. Use the steps of the book study method which you learned in this chapter. Summarize your study with a book chart and outline. Use the following form as a guide for this and future book studies. If the book contains more chapters than space provides on the form, you will need to use more than one form in order to complete your study.

BOOK STUDY CHART

Name Of Book: _____ Title For Chart: _____

Chapter Numbers

1	2	3	4	5	6	7	8	9	10	11	12	13	14	15	16	17	18

Chapter Titles

Author:

To:

Purpose:

Key Words:

Key Verse:

Characters:

Life And Ministry Principle

CHAPTER TWELVE

CHAPTER STUDY

OBJECTIVES:

Upon completion of this chapter you will be able to:

- Write the Key Verse from memory.
- List four steps in the chapter study method.
- Study the Bible by chapters.
- Create a chapter chart to summarize your studies.
- Create a chapter outline.

KEY VERSE:

> **Thy Word have I hid in mine heart, that I might not sin against thee.**
> **(Psalm 119:11)**

INTRODUCTION

In the last chapter you learned how to survey an entire book of the Bible. You will now learn how to study an individual chapter within a book of the Bible. An example of chapter study is provided and you are given the opportunity to do such a study in the "For Further Study" section of this lesson.

THE METHOD DEFINED

Chapter study is exactly what the title conveys. It is the study of God's Word chapter by chapter.

THE METHOD EXPLAINED

STEP ONE: SELECT A CHAPTER TITLE

Record on the Chapter Study Chart the name of the book and chapter number you are studying. Read the entire chapter and give it a title which reflects its content. (If you have done a book survey, you will have already selected a chapter title. Chapter Eleven on book study explains how to select chapter titles).

STEP TWO: MARK PARAGRAPH DIVISIONS

Mark the paragraph divisions within the chapter. In some Bibles the paragraphs are marked with a special paragraph mark (¶). In other Bibles they are marked with a boldface verse number. (Boldface means that the number is **darker** than the numbers in front of other verses.)

If your Bible has neither paragraph marks or boldface markings then you must determine the paragraph divisions yourself. To do this you must know the definition of a paragraph:

> "A paragraph is a group of verses which relate to the same subject matter. When the subject changes, then a new paragraph has begun."

Mark the paragraph divisions in your Bible by drawing a circle around the verse number where each paragraph begins.

STEP THREE: CREATE A CHAPTER STUDY CHART

On the Chapter Study Chart record the title of the chapter. List the verses of the paragraph divisions (see example). Then give each paragraph a title which reflects the content of that paragraph. Use the column with the heading "Notes" to record your thoughts about the relation between parts of the chapter (see example). These notes will assist you in creating the chapter outline.

STEP FOUR: CREATE A CHAPTER OUTLINE

In the last chapter you learned how to outline an entire book of the Bible. Now you will do a more detailed outline of one chapter. You already selected a title for the chapter when you did the chapter chart. Use this for the title of your outline.

Use the paragraph divisions and paragraph titles for the main points. Then select subpoints and outline the verses in each paragraph of the chapter. Record the verse numbers by the points and subpoints. Also include any other Bible references which relate to the subject and explain it more fully (see example). If the number of paragraphs exceeds the spaces on the chapter study form use additional forms. For long chapters in the Bible you may use several forms.

EXAMPLE OF THE METHOD

We have selected the book of Jude, which is a book with only one chapter, to use as an example of the chapter study method.

STEP ONE: SELECT A CHAPTER TITLE

The title selected for the one chapter in Jude is "Warning Against False Teachers."

STEP TWO: MARK PARAGRAPH DIVISIONS

The chapter was divided into paragraphs starting with verses 1, 3, 4, 5, 8, 11, 12, 14, 16, 17, 19, 20, 22, 24. These verses were circled in the Bible to mark the paragraph divisions.

STEP THREE: CREATE A CHAPTER STUDY CHART

Here is an example of a chapter study chart:

Chapter Study Chart

Book: Jude   Chapter: One   Chapter Title: Warning Against False Teachers

Verses	Paragraph Title	Notes
1-2	Introduction	Jude author
3	Purpose	Contend for faith
4	Certain Men	Five identifying characteristics
5-7	Historical Record	Israel, Angels, Sodom/Gomorrah
8-10	Description Begun	Five more characteristics
11	Description by Example	Cain, Balaam, Core
12-13	Description by Comparison	Spots in feasts, clouds, trees, waves, stars
14-15	Future Judgment	By Lord and saints, prophesied by Enoch
16	Description Continued	Five more characteristics
17-18	Remember the Words	Warning by Jesus
19	Description Continued	Three more characteristics
20-21	Avoiding Deception	A four point plan
22-23	How To Deal With Them	Two categories
24-25	Benediction	We can be kept from these evils

STEP FOUR: CREATE A CHAPTER OUTLINE

Here is the chapter outline we created from our study of Jude:

Chapter Outline Of Jude: Warning Against False Teachers

I. Introduction: Greeting 1:1-2

    A.   From: Jude
        1. Brother of James.
        2. Bond servant of Jesus Christ.
    B.   To:

        1. Sanctified by God.
        2. Preserved in Christ.
        3. Called.

II.   Purpose: 1:3

      A.   Original purpose: Common salvation.
      B.   Revised purpose: Exhortation that they earnestly contend for the faith.

III.   Characteristics of "certain men" (false teachers): 1:4

      A.   Crept in unawares.
      B.   Ordained to condemnation.
      C.   Ungodly men.
      D.   Turning God's grace to lasciviousness.
      E.   Denying the Lord Jesus Christ.

IV.   Three historical records: 1:5-7

      A.   Israel: Once saved, afterward destroyed: 5 (Numbers 13-14 and I Corinthians 10:5-10)
      B.   Angels: Left first estate, reserved in chains: 6 (II Peter 2:4)
      C.   Sodom and Gomorrah: Sin resulted in punishment by fire: 7 (Genesis 18-19)

V.   Description of false teachers 1:8-10 (continued description from verse 4)

      A.   Filthy dreamers: 8
      B.   Defile the flesh: 8
      C.   Despise dominion: 8
      D.   Speak evil of dignities: 8-9
          1.   Michael the archangel did not dare to speak evil even against the Devil.
          2.   These men speak evil of things they know not.
      E.   Corrupt natural things: 10

VI.   Description of these evil men by example: 1:11

      A.   Way of Cain: Rejected the blood as necessary for remission of sin. (Genesis 4)
      B.   Error of Balaam: Ministry for financial gain. (Numbers 22-24)
      C.   Gainsaying of Core: Denying God's designated leadership.(Numbers 16)

VII.   Description of these evil men by metaphor (comparison to natural examples) 1:12-13

      A.   Spots: Actually means "stones" in your feasts; stone in food.

B.   Clouds: Promising much but delivering nothing; easily driven this way and that.

C.   Trees: Without fruit, no roots or stability; twice dead: Once in sin and secondly in hypocrisy.

D.   Waves: Boisterous, noisy, but accomplishing nothing.

E.   Stars: Look bright, but reserved unto darkness.

VIII.   Future judgment prophesied by Enoch: 1:14-15 (Genesis 5:18-24)

A.   Judged by the Lord with 10,000 saints.

B.   For all their ungodly deeds committed.

C.   For all their hard speeches spoken against Him.

IX.   Description of evil men continued: 1:16-17

A.   Murmurers.

B.   Complainers.

C.   Walking after their own lusts.

D.   Mouth speaking swelling words (boasters).

E.   Have respect of persons, thinking some better than others because of wealth, position, etc.

X.   Remember: Jesus warned: 18-19

A.   Mockers would come in the last time.

B.   They would walk after their own ungodly lusts.

C.   They would separate themselves (groups, cliques).

D.   They would be sensual.

E.   They would not have the Spirit of God.

XI.   Four point plan for avoiding being deceived by these evil men: 1:20-21

A.   Build up yourself in the faith: 20

B.   Pray in the Holy Ghost: 20

C.   Keep yourself in the love of God: 21

D.   Look for the mercy of the Lord Jesus Christ: 21

XII.   Our response to these evil men: 1:22-23:

A.   On some have compassion: 22
      1.   Make a difference between these who are weak and the willfully evil (see following verse).

B.   Others save with fear: 23

1. Pull them out of the fire of sin/Hell.
2. Hate even the garments spotted by flesh.

XIII. Closing benediction: 1:24-25

    A. He is able to keep us from falling: 24
        1. To present us faultless.
        2. Before the presence of His glory.
        3. With exceeding great joy.
    B. To the only wise God our Savior, now and forever: 25
        1. Glory.
        2. Majesty.
        3. Dominion.
        4. Power.

USING QUESTIONS

Learning to ask questions will help you do detailed studies of Bible passages. The following list of questions concerns the one chapter of the book of Jude used as an example in this lesson. This list is an example of how learning to question can lead you into more detailed study of God's Word.

Verses 1-2:

Who is the author of the epistle?
What relationship to Jesus is stated?
What is the relationship to James?
What are the three ways in which Jude identifies his readers as Christians?
What does "kept" mean?
Since he is writing to those who are "kept" does this mean there are some who are called and beloved but not kept in Jesus?

Verse 3:

What does the "common salvation" mean?
What in Jude 3 indicates that the Holy Spirit changed Jude's mind about the subject of this letter?
What was he originally going to write about?
Who are the saints?

Verse 4:

Why is Jude warning them to contend for the faith?
What does "contend" mean?

Does the text indicate these false teachers would soon come or had already come?
Where had these ungodly men crept into?
What two words describe Jesus Christ?
What three things describe these ungodly men?

Verses 5-8:

What are the two facts about Israel mentioned in verse 5?
How do they relate to Jude's subject?
Who is the chief angel among those described in verse 6.
What is meant by the "great day"?
To what must "eternal fire" refer?

Verses 9-10:

Who was Michael?
Why did Michael not accuse the Devil?
What was the dispute between Michael and the Devil?
Who are the ones in verse 10 who speak evil?

Verse 11:

What three examples of punishment are given in this verse?
What was Cain's sin?
What was Balaam's sin?
What was Korah's sin?
What are the three words (verbs, action words) which describe the actions of the ungodly men?

Verses 12-13:

Jude compares these ungodly men with things from nature. What are they?
What is similar about the waves, clouds, and stars as described?

Verses 14-16:

Who was Enoch?
What in verse 16 might tempt a person to show respect of persons?

Verse 17-19:

What in verse 17 in similar to verse 1?
What is similar in verse 17 to verse 5?
How many times is the word "ungodly" used in verses 15 and 18?

Verse 20-23:

Who is responsible for having faith according to verse 20?
What does the word "building" infer as to the speed of attaining full maturity in Christian life?
Who is responsible for keeping us in the love of God?

Verses 24-25:

Who is able to keep us from falling?
What does it mean to be presented before God faultless?
What qualities of God are mentioned in verse 25?

SELF-TEST

1. Write the Key Verse from memory.

_____

_____

_____

2. What is the chapter study method of Bible study?

_____

_____

_____

3. List the four steps of the chapter study method of Bible study.

_____

_____

_____

_____

(Answers to tests are provided at the conclusion of the final chapter in this manual.)

FOR FURTHER STUDY

1. Use what you have learned in this chapter to do a study on II Peter 2. This chapter concerns the same subject as the chapter in Jude which was used as an example in this lesson.

Use the blank chapter study form provided on the next page. Make copies of this form to use in future chapter studies.

2. Make a list of questions from II Peter 2. This list will help you in the more detailed studies of paragraphs, verses, and words which you are to learn in the following chapters.

3. Read through the Gospels: Matthew, Mark, Luke, John. Write down all the questions asked by Jesus and observe how He used questions to help others learn.

CHAPTER STUDY

BOOK:_____

CHAPTER:_____

CHAPTER TITLE:_____

Verses	Paragraph Title	Notes

CHAPTER THIRTEEN

PARAGRAPH STUDY

OBJECTIVES:

Upon completion of this chapter you will be able to:

- Explain how to do a paragraph study.
- Do a paragraph study.
- Create a paragraph chart to summarize your studies.
- Outline a paragraph in the Bible.

KEY VERSE:

The entrance of thy words giveth light; it giveth understanding unto the simple. (Psalm 119:130)

INTRODUCTION

You have learned how to survey a book of the Bible and study a chapter within that book. When you studied a chapter you divided it into paragraphs. Now you will learn how to study the paragraphs. An example of paragraph study is provided and you are given the opportunity to do such a study in the "For Further Study" section of this lesson.

PARAGRAPH STUDY

STEP ONE: DO A CHAPTER STUDY:

As you have learned, each chapter of the Bible is composed of paragraphs. Paragraphs are groups of verses about the same subject. When the subject changes, a new paragraph begins. As you study a chapter you will note important paragraphs or paragraphs that seem to relate to one another. These are possibilities for paragraph studies.

STEP TWO: OBSERVE THE DETAILS:

The paragraphs in a chapter can relate to each other in different ways. Here are some special things to observe as you study paragraphs:

Connectives:

Words called "connectives" are very important. They reveal relationships within and between paragraphs. The word "but" is a connective and introduces a contrast. For example:

> **But these speak evil of those things which they know not; But what they know naturally, as brute beasts, in those things they corrupt themselves. (Jude 1:10)**

There is a contrast in this paragraph. False teachers speak evil of things they do not know BUT they also corrupt the things they do know. The verse begins with the word "but" which should make you look back to verse 9 to see what the contrast is:

> **Yet Michael the archangel, when contending with the devil he disputed about the body of Moses, durst not bring against him a railing accusation, but said, The Lord rebuke thee. (Jude 1:9)**

Verse 10 contrasts false teachers who speak evil of dignities with the archangel Michael. Even though he held a great position, he did not accuse the devil but said "The Lord rebuke thee." The connective word "or" indicates a contrast. For example:

> **For God shall bring every work into judgment, with every secret thing, whether it be good OR whether it be evil. (Ecclesiastes 12:14)**

Other connective words to watch for are "like" and "as." Instead of a contrast these words show comparisons between things. For example in the following verse Satan is compared to a lion:

> **. . . the Devil AS a roaring lion, walketh about, seeking whom he may devour. (I Peter 5:8)**

The word "and" is another connective. It adds to what has just been stated:

> **Like wise also these filthy dreamers defile the flesh, despise dominion, AND speak evil of dignities. (Jude 1:8)**

The word "if" introduces a conditional statement. Many of the promises and prophecies of the Old Testament are stated this way. They tell what God will do IF (on the condition that) His people make a certain response:

> **IF my people, which are called by my name, shall humble themselves, and pray, and seek my face, and turn from their wicked ways, then will I hear from Heaven and will forgive their sin, and will heal their land. (II Chronicles 7:14)**

The word "that" sets forth a purpose. It tells that something happened "in order that" a certain purpose would be accomplished:

> **And He came and dwelleth in a city called Nazareth; <u>THAT</u> it might be fulfilled which was spoken by the prophets, He shall be called a Nazarene. (Matthew 2:23)**

Watch also for the connecting words "for, because, therefore." These words introduce reasons and results:

> **But when He saw the multitudes, He was moved with compassion on them, <u>BECAUSE</u> they fainted, and were scattered abroad, as sheep having no shepherd. (Matthew 9:36)**

The words "in, into, and with" are also important connectives. They also indicate relationships between concepts:

> **He turned the sea <u>INTO</u> dry land and they went through the flood on foot: there did we rejoice in Him. (Psalm 66:6)**

General Structure:

As you study paragraphs observe the arrangement of ideas and how the verses relate to each other. Sometimes the author makes a general statement, then explains it with examples. Other times he lists a series of ideas and then summarizes with a general statement.

In the example given later in this chapter, you will note that Jude wrote several paragraphs listing characteristics of false teachers. He then gave Old Testament examples which illustrated what he was teaching.

Repetitions:

Each word of the Bible is inspired by the Holy Spirit. When words or phrases are repeated it is because they are especially important. The Holy Spirit inspired the writers to repeat words and phrases in order to fix them in your memory.

The words "verily, verily" are an example of this. When Jesus preceded a statement with these words it was like an announcer saying "May I have your attention please. I have an important announcement to make." Study in detail any words, phrases, or verses that are repeated.

Questions And Answers:

It is also important to observe the questions and answers of the Bible. Often an author will introduce a subject by asking a question. He will then explain this question and give answers which relate back to the question. A good example of this is Romans 6. Read the entire chapter. Note the questions in verses 1-3 and the answers developed throughout the chapter.

Introductions:

Watch for paragraphs that introduce the subject that is to follow. For example, in the book of Jude which you studied in the last chapter verse 3 introduces the material to follow:

> **Beloved, when I gave all diligence to write unto you of the common salvation, it was needful for me to write unto you, and exhort you, that ye should earnestly contend for the faith which was once delivered unto the saints. (Jude 1:3)**

This introductory paragraph explains the purpose of his writing. He is exhorting them to earnestly contend for the true faith. The remainder of the chapter gives reasons for this exhortation. There are false teachers creeping into the church who are trying to turn them from the true faith.

Summaries And Conclusions:

Be alert for paragraphs that summarize an entire passage, chapter, or even a book. For example, the book of Ecclesiastes contains one verse which summarizes the whole book. In Ecclesiastes the writer has described his quest for life apart from God. His final conclusion is:

> **Let us hear the conclusion of the whole matter: Fear God, and keep His commandments: for this is the whole duty of man.**
>
> **For God shall bring every work into judgment, with every secret thing, whether it be good, or whether it be evil. (Ecclesiastes 12:13-14)**

Progressions In Thought:

When studying paragraphs, watch for progressions in thought. Note the following paragraph:

> **And beside this, giving all diligence, add to your faith virtue; and to virtue knowledge;**
>
> **And to knowledge temperance; and to temperance patience; and to patience godliness;**
>
> **And to godliness brotherly kindness; and to brotherly kindness charity.**
>
> **For if these things be in you and abound, they make you that ye shall neither**

be barren or unfruitful in the knowledge of our Lord Jesus Christ.

But he that lacketh these things is blind, and cannot see afar off, and hath forgotten that he was purged from his old sins. (II Peter 1:5-9)

There is definite progression in this passage. We are to add one thing to another until we become fruitful.

Literary Form:

Literary form refers to how a passage is written. Some passages are in narrative or story form. This means they read like a story. Other paragraphs are in poetic form (poems) like the passages in the book of Psalms. Some paragraphs are parables which are short stories illustrating a spiritual truth. Some paragraphs are in dramatic form. For example, the Song of Solomon contains dramatic as well as poetic form. Discourse form is much like a sermon. It is a series of paragraphs giving instruction on a certain subject.

Key Words:

Identifying key words will help you understand the meaning of a paragraph. Key words are those important to the meaning of a paragraph. Often they are words which are repeated. Especially note key words which you do not understand. These words can be studied in a word study. (You will learn how to do this later in this course). For example, read the following verse:

For there are certain men crept in unawares, who were before of old ordained to this condemnation, ungodly men, turning the grace of our God into lasciviousness, and denying the only Lord God and our Lord Jesus Christ. (Jude 1:4)

Do you know what the word "lasciviousness" means? It is an important word in this paragraph because it describes false teachers. One of their characteristics is that they have turned the grace of God into lasciviousness. This word is an example of a key word to study.

Grammatical Construction:

The word "grammar" refers to parts of speech or words that fit together to make up sentences and paragraphs. Watch for words which are called verbs. These are words that show action telling what someone did in the past, is doing in the present, or will do in the future. They also are used in commands:

GO ye into all the world and PREACH the Gospel to every creature. (Mark 16:15)

The words "go" and "preach" are action words. They are verbs. They are commands for us to obey. A noun is a word that names a person, place, or thing. The words in capitals below are nouns:

JUDE, the servant of JESUS CHRIST, and brother of JAMES... (Jude 1:1)

Nouns tell who and what is involved and where the action took place. A pronoun is a word that replaces or stands for a noun. The words "him" and "her" are examples. Instead of saying "The Holy Spirit inspired Jude to write the book" you could say "The Holy Spirit inspired HIM to write the book." The word "him" is a pronoun standing for the noun Jude.

Adjectives and adverbs are important parts of speech also. Adverbs tell something about a verb. It tells how something happened. For example, in the sentence "He ran quickly," the word "quickly" is an adverb because it tells how he ran. An adjective describes a noun or pronoun. If we said "Jude was tall," the word "tall" is an adjective which describes Jude.

If you have not studied parts of speech before this may seem confusing at first, but you will soon learn to identify these as you practice. Parts of speech are important because they identify people, places, and things. They tell who did something, where, when, and why. They tell how things were done and what was, is, or will be done. They also provide descriptions and details which increase understanding of the subject matter.

STEP THREE: CREATE A PARAGRAPH STUDY CHART:

By studying paragraphs in detail as described in Step Two, you will identify certain paragraphs that relate to each other. Their relationship may be contrasts, comparisons, progressions, or otherwise. Select these for paragraph study.

You will create a chart to summarize your study of these paragraphs. Select a general title for your chart which reflects the relationship of the paragraphs or the subject which they concern. The chart will also include the paragraph titles and divisions made during the chapter study. Record on the chart the book, chapter, and paragraphs studied. Use margins of the chart to make observations and applications.

STEP FOUR: CREATE A PARAGRAPH OUTLINE:

Use the chart to help you create an outline of the paragraphs. The outlines you create on chapters and paragraphs will help you as you share God's truth with others because they help you present what you have learned in an orderly way.

EXAMPLE OF THE METHOD

STEP ONE: DO A CHAPTER STUDY:

A chapter study of Jude 1 was done in the previous lesson. We will do the paragraph study from this same chapter, so we have already completed Step One.

STEP TWO: OBSERVE THE DETAILS:

As the paragraphs of Jude 1 were studied in depth, relationships emerged between paragraphs 4, 8-10, 16, 17-18, and 19. These paragraphs all list characteristics of false teachers.

STEP THREE: CREATE A PARAGRAPH STUDY CHART:

In previous chapters we provided a blank chart for your studies. For paragraph studies you will draw your own chart because it is not possible to determine the proper space to leave on a chart for paragraph studies. This is the reason why we did not create a standard form. Some paragraphs are very detailed and require more space for study notes.

An example of a Paragraph Study Chart follows. Use this example to create your own study chart. Be sure to put the verse numbers of each paragraph in the paragraph block (note number in upper left of each block division on the chart).

Paragraph Study Chart

Book: Jude   Chapter: 1   Paragraphs: 4, 8-10, 16, 17-18, 19

Title: Characteristics Of False Teachers

4

Crept in unawares	Walk
Before of old ordained to this condemnation	Background
Ungodly men	Conduct
Turning the grace of our God into lasciviousness	Doctrine
Denying the only Lord God and our Lord Jesus Christ	Doctrine

8-10

Filthy dreamers	Conduct
Defile the flesh	Conduct
Despise dominion	Conduct
Speak evil of dignities	Talk
Speak evil of things they know not	Talk
What they know naturally they corrupt	Conduct

16

Murmurers	Talk
Complainers	Talk
Walking after their own lusts	Walk
Mouth speaks great swelling words	Talk
Have men's persons in admiration because of advantage	Conduct

18

Mockers	Talk
Walk after their own ungodly lusts	Walk
Separate themselves	Conduct
Sensual	Conduct
Have not the Spirit	Doctrine

Key words to study:

Lasciviousness (paragraph 4): What does this word mean?

144

STEP FOUR: CREATE A PARAGRAPH OUTLINE:

Here is an outline of the paragraph on "Characteristics Of False Teachers."

I.   Their background:

      A. Before of old ordained to this condemnation.

II.   Their walk:

      A. Crept in unawares.
      B. Walking after their own lusts.
      C. Walking after their own ungodly lusts.

III.   Their talk:

      A. Speak evil of dignities.
      B. Speak evil of things they know not.
      C. Murmurers.
      D. Complainers.
      E. Mouths speak great swelling words.
      F. Mockers.

IV.   Their doctrine:

      A. Turn the grace of God into lasciviousness.
      B. Deny the only Lord God and our Lord Jesus Christ.
      C. Have not the Spirit.

V.   Their conduct:

      A. Ungodly.
      B. Filthy dreamers.
      C. Defile the flesh.
      D. Sensual.
      E. Separate themselves.
      F. Corrupt natural knowledge.
      G. Despise dominion.
      H. Partiality based on position of men.

SELF-TEST

1. Write the Key Verse from memory.

_____

_____

_____

2. List the four steps of the paragraph study method.

_____

_____

_____

3. Look at the name of the literary form in List One. Read the definitions in List Two. Write the number of the definition in front of the literary form which it describes.

List One

_____ Discourse

_____ Poetic

_____ Parable

_____ Narrative

List Two

1. Story form

2. Poetry: Psalms is an example

3. Like a sermon

4. Short stories to illustrate spiritual truth

4. Look at the name of the part of speech in List One. Read the definitions in List Two. Write the number of the definition in front of the part of speech which it describes:

List One   **List Two**

_____Noun   1. An action word.

_____Pronoun   2. Tells how something was done.

_____Verb   3. A descriptive word.

_____Adverb   4. Name of a person, place, or thing.

_____Adjective   5. You use this in place of the name of a person.

5. Look at the connective words in List One. Read the definitions in List Two. Write the number of the definition in front of the words it describes.

List One   **List Two**

_____Like, As   1. These words show a contrast is going to be made.

_____And   2. This word means something is going to be added to what has been said.

_____If   3. These words reveal that a comparison is going to be made.

_____But, or   4. This word shows that what has conditional upon the response of God's people.

(Answers to tests are provided at the conclusion of the final chapter in this manual.)

FOR FURTHER STUDY

1. Do a paragraph study on Jude chapter 1 paragraphs 5-7, 11, and 12- 13 of Jude chapter 1.

These paragraphs all are "Examples Of False Teachers." This should be the title of your chart.

Verses 5-7 give an example of the judgment on false teachers.

Verse 11 gives examples of their errors.

Verses 12-13 give natural examples (comparisons) of false teachers.

2. In the preceding chapter you did a chapter study on II Peter chapter 2. The subject of this chapter is similar to Jude 1. It concerns false teachers. Now do a paragraph study on II Peter 2. Perhaps you can add to the charts already started--"Characteristics Of False Teachers" and "Examples Of False Teachers."

CHAPTER FOURTEEN

VERSE STUDY

OBJECTIVES:

Upon completion of this chapter you will be able to:

- Write the Key Verse from memory.
- Explain how to do a verse study.
- Do a verse study.
- Create a chart to summarize your verse study.
- Create a verse study outline.

KEY VERSE:

> **My tongue shall speak of thy Word: for all thy commandments are righteousness. (Psalm 119:172)**

INTRODUCTION

You learned how to survey a Bible book and do a chapter study within that book. You also learned how to study the paragraphs within a chapter. In this lesson you will learn how to study a single verse in detail. An example is provided and you are given an opportunity to do a verse study in the "For Further Study" section of this chapter.   As you do a verse study, use all you have learned in previous lessons about questioning and examining details of structure.

THE METHOD DEFINED

STEP ONE: STUDY THE VERSE WITHIN ITS CONTEXT:

Each verse must be interpreted within its context. The context is the surrounding verses of the passage where it is located. The context gives a complete message from God of which one verse is only a part. It is important that a single verse is not taken out of context and misinterpreted. This is often the practice of false teachers.

STEP TWO: STUDY RELATED VERSES:

Within the context you will discover verses related to the one you have selected for study. They will add more information to the verse you are studying.   They may provide a contrast or comparison. Sometimes the verse you are studying may relate to verses in another book of the Bible. (See the example in this chapter). Look up these references and study them also.

STEP THREE: CREATE A VERSE STUDY CHART:

Select a title for the chart. On the verse study chart record the name of the book, chapter number, and verse number which you are studying. How you organize your chart will depend on the type of information you accumulate in your study. If you have completed the "For Further Study" assignments in previous chapters you have enough experience with study charts that you will be able to create your own original charts. You may use either a horizontal or vertical chart depending on the information you are recording.

STEP FOUR: CREATE A VERSE STUDY OUTLINE:

Using the outlining skills you have developed in previous assignments, create an outline of the verse. Select an appropriate title, main headings, and subheadings. Use your chart to help you prepare the outline of the verse.

EXAMPLE OF THE METHOD

STEP ONE: STUDY THE VERSE WITHIN ITS CONTEXT

We selected Jude 1:11 as the verse to demonstrate the verse study method. In previous lessons we studied this verse in its chapter and paragraph settings so we have already completed the study of the verse within its context. When you select a verse for study examine it within its context first. You do this by chapter and paragraph study, skills which you learned in the previous two lessons. Also remember to consider the verse within the larger framework of the entire book in which it is located. The study of Jude 1:11 within its context is recorded on the Verse Study Chart.

STEP TWO: STUDY RELATED VERSES:

Jude 1:11 is related to other verses about false teachers in chapter one. Verses 5-7 give historical examples and verses 12-13 give natural examples of false teachers. Jude 1:11 is also related to three important Old Testament passages:

The story of Cain:	Genesis 4:1-15; I John 3:12
The story of Balaam:	Numbers 22-24
The story of Core:	Numbers 16

The study of these related verses are recorded on the summarizing chart and in the outline.

STEP THREE: CREATE A VERSE STUDY CHART:

Study the example of the verse study chart which follows:

VERSE STUDY CHART

Book: Jude   Chapter: 1   Verse: 11

OLD TESTAMENT EXAMPLES OF FALSE TEACHERS
Jude 1:11: GOD SAYS: WOE TO THEM

THE REASONS...

1. They have gone in the way of CAIN
   Genesis 4:1-15: He denied the plan of God that only through the shedding
   of blood are sins forgiven. See Hebrews 9:22
   I John 3:12: He slew his brother because his own works were evil.

2. They ran greedily after the error of BALAAM
   Numbers 22-24 Did anything for financial benefit.

3. They perished in the gainsaying of CORE (Korah)
   Numbers 16: Denied the authority of God's chosen leadership.

Note the progression: They HAVE GONE the wrong way....
                                  Then they RUN GREEDILY after error...
                                    They PERISH......

Other examples of false teachers in Jude 1:
Historical examples: Verses 5-7
Natural examples: Verses 12-13

STEP FOUR: CREATE A VERSE STUDY OUTLINE:

Here is an example of an outline of a verse:

OLD TESTAMENT EXAMPLES OF FALSE TEACHERS

Book: Jude   Chapter: 1   Verse: 11

I.   God says woe to them (false teachers).

II.   The reasons:
    A.   They have gone in the way of Cain:
        1.   Genesis 4:1-15 He denied the plan of God that only through the shedding of blood are sins forgiven.
            a.   This truth is expressed in Hebrews 9:22.
        2.   I John 3:12: He slew his brother because his own works were evil.
    B.   They ran greedily after the error of Balaam.
        1.   Numbers 22-24:   Balaam did anything for financial benefit.
    C.   They perished in the gainsaying of Core (Old Testament spelling is Korah)
        1.   Numbers 16:   Korah denied the authority of God's chosen leadership.

III.   There is a progression of evil:
    A.   First, we go the wrong way.
    B.   Soon we are running greedily in error.
    C.   The end result is perishing.

IV.   Other examples of false teachers in Jude 1:
    A.   Historical examples: Verses 5-7
        1.   Israel
        2.   Angels
        3.   Sodom and Gomorrah
    B.   Natural examples: Verses 12-13
        1.   Spots in feasts.
        2.   Clouds without water.
        3.   Trees without fruit.
        4.   Raging waves.
        5.   Wandering stars.

Note: Remember, as in all Bible study methods, it is important that you apply what you have learned in verse study. How does the verse you studied apply to your life and ministry? Review the "Devotional Method" for guidelines of application.

SELF-TEST

1. Write the Key Verse from memory.

_____

_____

_____

2. It is important that we always study a verse within its...

_____

3. List the four steps of the Verse Study Method.

_____

_____

_____

_____

(Answers to tests are provided at the conclusion of the final chapter in this manual.)

FOR FURTHER STUDY

In previous lessons you completed a book survey, chapter study, and paragraph study.

Select a verse from a paragraph which you previously studied. Using the skills you learned in this chapter do a verse study. Summarize your study with a Verse Study Chart and outline in the space provided below.

VERSE STUDY CHART:

VERSE OUTLINE:

CHAPTER FIFTEEN

WORD STUDY

OBJECTIVES:

Upon completion of this chapter you will be able to:

- Write the Key Verse from memory.
- Identify key Bible words for study.
- Explain how to do a Bible word study.
- Do a Bible word study.

KEY VERSE:

> **For verily I say unto you, Till Heaven and earth pass, one jot or one tittle shall in no wise pass from the law, till all be fulfilled. (Matthew 5:18)**

INTRODUCTION

You have learned how to study the Bible by books, chapters, paragraphs, and verses. In this lesson you will learn how to study the smallest unit of the Bible which is a single word. An example of the word study method is presented and you are given an opportunity to do such a study in the "For Further Study" section of this chapter.

THE METHOD DEFINED

Word study is the study of individual words in the Bible. The goal of word study is to understand a word in its context. Each detail of the inspired Word is so important that Jesus said:

> **For verily I say unto you, Till Heaven and earth pass. one jot or one tittle shall in no wise pass from the law, till all be fulfilled. (Matthew 5:18)**

"Jots and tittles" were Hebrew letters. If even these were emphasized by Jesus, then we know that every word of God is important. The meaning of individual words affects the meaning of verses. Verses explain paragraphs. Paragraphs help you understand chapters and chapters provide knowledge of an entire book.

The following diagram illustrates Bible structure from general (book) to specific (verse).

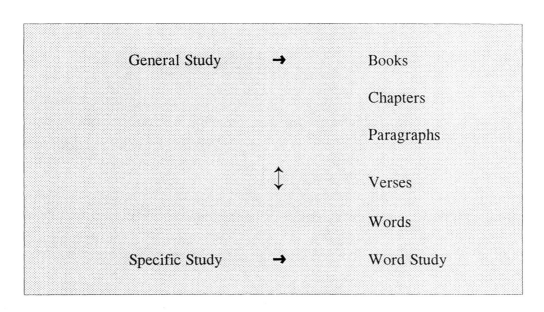

General Study → Books

Chapters

Paragraphs

↕ Verses

Words

Specific Study → Word Study

THE METHOD EXPLAINED

STEP ONE: SELECT THE WORD

During the studies of chapters, paragraphs, and verses, we introduced the concept of key words. A key word is one that is basic to the meaning of a verse. It is an important word. Sometimes it is a word that is repeated for special emphasis or a word that is difficult to understand.

Care must be taken in selecting a word to study. For example, words such as "to, and, if," are not key words. They are connective words and add meaning, but they are not good words to use for word study. Be sure the word you select for study is a key word.

STEP TWO: STUDY THE WORD WITHIN ITS CONTEXT

Study the word within the context of the chapter. Is the word repeated elsewhere in the chapter? If so, what is revealed about its meaning? Is there another verse in the chapter that explains the meaning of the word? Next, study the word within the context of the paragraph. What is the subject of the paragraph? How does this key word relate to the subject?

Then study the word within the context of the verse. How does it relate to the verse? What part of speech is the word: Is it a noun, pronoun, verb, adverb, or adjective?

If you select a word to study and have not previously analyzed the context in which it appears, you must always take time to do this. Chapters, paragraphs, verses, and words all fit together to provide complete understanding of God's Word. It is important that a word or verse is not taken out of context because you might interpret it incorrectly.

STEP THREE: DETERMINE THE MEANING OF THE WORD

After selecting a key word and studying its context, the next step is to determine the meaning of the word.

Watch for words which are different but have the same meaning, for example, "Kingdom of God" and "Kingdom of Heaven." Watch for words which are the same but have different meanings. For example, in John 21:15-17 Jesus asked Peter three times, "Lovest thou me more than these?" Each time the meaning of the word "love" was different.

Unless you know Greek or Hebrew and have a Bible in these languages you will not be able to determine the original meaning of the word without additional study tools. The two basic study helps you need are a concordance and a Bible word study book. Chapter Five of this manual explains how to use both of these Bible study tools.

If you do not have a concordance or word study book you can still study a Bible word even though you may not be able to trace the original meaning. IF YOU DO NOT have a concordance or Bible word study book, then follow these steps:

    1. If your Bible has a center margin which lists additional references for study, look up all the verses listed. They may expand your understanding of the word. Sometimes the center margin actually gives the meaning of the word.

    2. Check in the back of your Bible. Some Bibles have a small concordance which lists some of the most important words. Some Bibles also have a dictionary in the back which provides definitions.

    3. Look up the word in a modern language dictionary. This will provide knowledge of the current meaning of the word even though the way it was used in Bible days may have been somewhat different.

    4. Study other uses of the word in the chapter or book. This will also help determine the meaning of the word.

IF YOU DO have a concordance and/or Bible word study book, then follow these steps:

    1. If your Bible has a center margin which gives additional references and word meanings, see if the word you are studying is listed. (Point 1 in the preceding section explains how to use the center margin of your Bible).

    2. Look up the word in a Bible concordance. Words are listed in a concordance in

alphabetical order. If the word is used several places in the Bible, you will find a list of verses which contain the word. Study these verses to help you understand the meaning.

Find the word as it is used in the verse you are studying. Note the number given at the end of the concordance listing and look up this number in the back of the concordance. If you are studying a word from a verse in the Old Testament you will look up the number in the Hebrew Dictionary. If you are studying a word from the New Testament you will look up the word in the Greek Dictionary. (Chapter Five explains how to do this.)

When you find the word number, it gives you the original meaning of the word in Greek or Hebrew. It may also refer you to another number in the dictionary. This means the word you are studying came from another word. To trace your word back to the original meaning you will have to look up this other word also.

3. Look up the word in a Bible word study book. Words are listed in alphabetical order in a word study book. If your word is used elsewhere in the Bible you will find several listings. While you want to study these also, be sure to pay special attention to the verse from which you have selected your word. Your purpose is to determine what this word means within the context of that particular verse.

4. Look up the word in a regular dictionary. This will tell you how the word is currently used in modern language. It may be similar to its use in the Bible or it may be quite different. The difference between the use of words in modern language and in the Bible results from two things:

First, the meanings of words change throughout time. New meanings are attached to old words and sometimes the original meanings are forgotten.

Second, the Bible was written in Greek and Hebrew. The same word has different meanings in different languages. The word meant one thing in Greek or Hebrew but may be different in another language.

STEP FOUR: SUMMARIZE YOUR STUDY

During the first three steps of word study make notes on what you learn about the word. Write down the meanings of the word from the Bible margin, concordance, word study book, and modern dictionary. Record notes on its use in other Bible passages.

When you complete your study, use what you have learned about charts and outlines to summarize your word study notes. Remember to record somewhere on your chart or outline the book, chapter, verse number, and word you are studying.

EXAMPLE OF THE METHOD

STEP ONE: SELECT THE WORD

In previous lessons we used Jude chapter 1 to demonstrate the methods of chapter, paragraph, and verse studies. From our study of Jude 1 we have selected the word "lasciviousness" in verse 4. This word is a key word because it describes false teachers which is the subject of this chapter. It is also a key word because it is a word that is difficult to understand.

STEP TWO: STUDY THE WORD WITHIN ITS CONTEXT

In previous lessons you completed a chapter and paragraph study on the book of Jude. This means you have already studied the word lasciviousness within these contexts. You learned that the subject of Jude 1 is a warning against false teachers. Verse 4, in which the word lasciviousness is used is one of the paragraphs of Jude 1. Refer to the lessons on chapter and paragraph studies to study this word within these contexts.

In the last chapter we explained how to do a verse study. You have not yet done a verse study on Jude 1:4 where the word lasciviousness appears. Stop now and do a verse study on Jude 1:4 before you continue this lesson on word studies.

In your verse study you should have identified the word lasciviousness as an adjective because it is a descriptive word that describes false teachers. False teachers turn the grace of God into lasciviousness.

STEP THREE: DETERMINE THE MEANING OF THE WORD

1. The Bible we were using for study of the word lasciviousness in Jude 1:4 had a center margin. The center margin referred us to Titus 2:11 and Hebrews 12:15.

2. Here is the concordance listing for the word lasciviousness:

Lasciviousness		
wickedness, deceit, l, an evil. . . . . .Mk 7:22	766
l which they have committed. . . . . .2 Cor 12:21	766
fornication, uncleanness, l. . . . . Gal 5:19	766
have given themselves over unto l. . . . . Eph 4:19	766
the Gentiles, when we walked in l. . . . . 1 Pet 4:3	766
the grace of our God into l. . . . . .Jude 4	766

All the verses where the word was used were looked up and studied. The number "766" appears at the end of the listing for Jude 1:4. This is the same number at the end of the other listings. This means that the word lasciviousness has the same meaning in all the texts listed.

Since lasciviousness is a word in the New Testament, we used the Greek dictionary in the back of the concordance to look up number 766. This is the listing from the Greek dictionary:

> 766. Aselgeia, from a comp. Of I (as a neg. Particle) and a presumed selges (of uncertain der., but apparently, mean continent); licentiousness (sometimes including other vices):-filthy, lasciviousness, wantonness.

3. A Bible word study book was then used. Below is the listing for "lasciviousness":

> **Lascivious, Lasciviousness**
>
> Aselegeia denotes excess, licentiousness, absences of restraint, indecency, wantonness; in Mark 7:22, one of the evils that proceed from the heart; in 2 Cor 12:21, one of the evils of which some in the church at Corinth had been guilty; in Gal 5:19, classed among the works of the flesh; in Eph 4:19, among the sins of the unregenerate who are past feeling; so in I Pet 4:3; in Jude 4, of that into which the grace of God had been turned by ungodly men; it is translated "wantonness" in Rom 13:13, one of the sins against which believers are warned.

We studied this entire listing, with special attention to the word as used in Jude 1:4.

4. A regular dictionary gave the modern meaning for the word lasciviousness:

"Lewd, lustful, exciting, sensual emotions."

STEP FOUR: SUMMARIZE YOUR STUDY

During the previous steps we made notes as we studied the word lasciviousness.

In <u>Step One</u> we wrote down the word selected for study.

In <u>Step Two</u> we already had chapter and paragraph studies from previous lessons. These became part of our word study. You were asked to do the verse study on Jude 1:4. All the information from these studies become part of the word study notes.

In <u>Step Three</u> as we studied the Bible margin, concordance, word study book, current dictionary, and other references containing the word, we took notes on what we were learning about the word lasciviousness.

We collected quite a bit of information about this word. The final step in our study is to summarize this material in chart and/or outline form. As we learned in previous lessons this is the best way to save studies in an organized way. It also helps you share what you learn with others.

The following pages presents the summary of our word study on lasciviousness. Use these as examples of how to summarize your own word studies through charts and outlines, even pictures or diagrams.

As with each previous method discussed, we want to remind you of the importance of applying what you learn through word study. Bible study is not a quest for knowledge in itself. You must be a doer or the word and not a hearer only. You do this through applying the truths of God's Word.

WORD STUDY

Book: Jude
Chapter: 1
Verse: 4
Word: lasciviousness

Other words which have the same meaning: Wantonness

Part of Speech: Lasciviousness is an adjective. In Jude 1:4 it is used to describe a characteristic of false teachers.

Chart One

Lasciviousness: Definitions

Reference Book	Word Number	Spelling	Meaning
Greek	766	aselgeia	licentiousness, filthy, wantonness.
Modern	---	lasciviousness	lewd, lustful, exciting sensual emotions.
Vine's Word Study	___	aselgeia	denotes excess, absence of restraint, indecency wantonness.

Chart Two

Lasciviousness: Additional Bible Uses

Reference	Summary
Mark 7:22	It is an evil that proceeds from the heart.
II Corinthians 12:21	It was one of the evils of which some in the at Corinth had been guilty
Galatians 5:19	Listed among the works of the flesh.
Ephesians 4:19	One of the sins of the unregenerate who are past feeling
I Peter 4:3	One of the sins of the unregenerate who are past feeling
Romans 13:13	Word is translated "wantonness" and is one sins against which believers are warned.
II Peter 2:2	It is translated "wantonness" and is listed as the characteristics of false teachers
Jude 1:4	It is a characteristic of false teachers

Lasciviousness Expanded Studies

Word studies can lead to additional expanded studies of God's Word.   From the study of the word lasciviousness, the following additional studies could be made:

1. Study the word in Mark 7:22 where it is listed as a sin which comes from within. What other sins come from within?

2. Study II Corinthians 12:21. What other sins besides lasciviousness did Paul identify in the Corinthian church?

3. Look up the word "wantonness" in the concordance. This word means the same as lasciviousness. Are there other Bible uses of the word "wantonness"?

4. Galatians 5:19. What are the other works of the flesh besides lasciviousness?

5. Ephesians 4. Study verses 17-19. Prepare a chart contrasting unbelievers and believers. List the characteristics of unbelievers given in verses 17-19. These include lasciviousness. List the characteristics of believers in verses 20-24.

6. Study I Peter 4:3. What were some of the other sins besides lasciviousness in which we walked in times past?

7. Study Romans 13:13. In addition to "wantonness" which means lasciviousness, what are other sins in which a believer should not engage?

8. Study the grace of God which false teachers have turned into lasciviousness. For example, Titus 2:11 says the grace of God has appeared to all men. Hebrews 12:15 indicates that we can "fail of the grace of God."

SELF-TEST

1. Write the Key Verse from memory.

_____

_____

_____

2. List the four steps of the word study method.

_____

_____

_____

_____

3. What is a key word?

_____

4. Which word in the list below is a key word and would be a good subject for word

study?_____

he   temperance   she   if   and

5. What are the two most important Bible study books to use in doing word studies?

_____

_____

(Answers to tests are provided at the conclusion of the final chapter in this manual.)

FOR FURTHER STUDY

Select a word from a verse or paragraph which you studied in previous lessons. Be sure it is a key word or a word you do not understand. Using the skills you learned in this lesson, do a word study on the word you selected.

STEP ONE: SELECT THE WORD

The word I have selected to study is:_____

STEP TWO: STUDY THE WORD WITHIN ITS CONTEXT

The Scriptural references for this word in its context are:

_____

_____

_____

STEP THREE: DETERMINE THE MEANING OF THE WORD

As used in this context, this word means:

_____

_____

_____

_____

_____

_____

STEP FOUR: SUMMARIZE YOUR STUDY

Create a chart, outline, picture, or diagram to summarize what you learned about this word.

CHAPTER SIXTEEN

TOPICAL BIBLE STUDY

OBJECTIVES:

Upon completion of this chapter you will be able to:

*   Write the Key Verses from memory.
*   Explain the topical method of Bible study.
*   Do a topical Bible study.

KEY VERSES:

> Therefore I love thy commandments above gold; yea, above fine gold.
>
> Therefore I esteem all thy precepts concerning all things to be right: and I hate every false way. (Psalm 119:127-128)

INTRODUCTION

This chapter introduces the topical method of Bible study. The method is defined and explained and an example of a topical study is provided. The "For Further Study" section provides an opportunity to apply what you have learned by actually doing a topical Bible study.

THE METHOD DEFINED

The topical method focuses on a selected Biblical subject. The goal of the study is to discover all the Bible teaches on the subject.

THE METHOD EXPLAINED

Here are the steps for doing a topical Bible study:

STEP ONE: SELECT A TOPIC:

You may choose a <u>general</u> subject, for example, all of the miracles in the Bible. You may select a more <u>specific</u> subject such as the miracles performed by Jesus or the miracles recorded in a certain book of the Bible.

For your first study it is best to limit the topic to a specific subject in one book rather than study a subject in the entire Bible. You may select a topic which pertains to a need in your own life. You might select a topic about which you have been asked and could not answer or a topic which you do not fully understand.

You may want to study topics you can use in counseling others in time of need. For example, you may want to study the topic of death so you will know how to comfort others. Or you may want to study fear so you can help those who are fearful.

STEP TWO: SELECT THE PORTION OF SCRIPTURE:

After choosing a topic, select the portion of Scripture in which you will study this topic. You can study a topic in one book of the Bible, several books, or the entire Bible.

STEP THREE: GATHER THE INFORMATION:

Find all the verses which relate to the topic in the portion of Scripture you select to study. A concordance is helpful but not necessary. For example, if you are studying the miracles of Jesus, read the books of Matthew, Mark, Luke, and John. Record each reference to a miracle performed by Jesus.

STEP FOUR: SUMMARIZE THE INFORMATION:

After you gather all the information on a topic you will probably have a long list of Scriptures. You must now organize these verses to make the subject easily understood.

Study the verses you collected. Identify main points made by the verses. What other verses make this same point? Arrange these verses together, then create a chart or outline to summarize your studies.

Remember: You not only want to learn all the Bible teaches about a specific topic, but you also want to apply what you learn to your own life and ministry.

EXAMPLE OF THE METHOD

STEP ONE: SELECT A TOPIC:

Miracles

STEP TWO: SELECT THE PORTION OF SCRIPTURE:

Miracles in the book of Luke will be studied.

STEP THREE: GATHER THE INFORMATION:

Miracles in Luke: 1:11, 3:21, 4:30, 5:1, 7:11, 9:28, 10:17, 4:33, 13:11, 14:1, 17:11, 22:50

STEP FOUR: SUMMARIZE THE INFORMATION:

Example of an outline summary:

<u>Miracles In The Book Of Luke</u>

I.   Thirty one miracles are recorded in the book of Luke.

II.   People who performed them:

      A.   The Lord Jesus Christ: 4:28-30; 4:31-37; 4:38-39; 4:40-41; 5:1-11; 5:12-15; 5:17-26; 6:6-11; 6:17-20; 7:1-10; 7:11-15; 7:21; 8:2-3; 8:22-25; 8:26-39; 8:41-42, 49, 56; 8:43-48; 9:11-17; 9:37-43; 11:14-23; 13:10-17; 14:1-6; 17:11-19; 18:35-43; 22:50-51; 24:1-7; 24:50-51.

      B.   Others:

            1.   Angel Gabriel: 1:11-23, 57,59
            2.   Holy Ghost: 3:21-22
            3.   God: 9:28-37
            4.   Disciples: 10:17

III.   Classification of miracles:

      A.   Raising the dead: 7:11-15; 8:41-42, 49, 56; 24:1-7

      B.   Casting out demons: 4:33-37; 8:2-3; 8:26-39; 9:14-23; 9:37-43

      C.   Healing: 4:38-39; 4:40-41; 5:12-16; 5:17-26; 6:6-10;6:17-20; 7:1-10; 8:43-48; 13:11-17; 14:1-6; 17:11-19;18:35-43; 22:50-51.

      D.   Over the forces of nature: 5:1-11; 8:22-25; 9:11-17

Example Of A Chart Summary:

A chart summary can also be done on each miracle in the book of Luke. The chart could include the following headings:

Miracle: What the miracle was, reference.
Realm: Was it a miracle over nature, healing, raising of the dead, casting out demons, etc?
Occasion: On what occasion was the miracle performed?
People: What people were involved?
Method: What method was used? Was it the spoken word, a touch, a prayer, etc.?
Results: What were the results of the miracle?
Reactions: What were the reactions of the people who witnessed or were part of the miracle?

An example of the analysis of one miracle is shown on the following chart. Such a study could be done on each miracle in the book of Luke.

Miracles In The Book Of Luke

Miracle	Realm	Occasion	People	Means	Results	Reactions
Healing	Physical	At home of Peter's Mother-in-law	Peter, and his Mother-in-law	Rebuke	Fever left	She arose, and ministered to others

The previous chart is designed specifically to study miracles and cannot be used for other topics, but it serves as an example of how you can create your own charts to summarize topical Bible studies. Here are some examples of just a few of the life and ministry applications which can be made from this study. Can you think of others?

-Are miracles to be part of the ministry of believers? (See Matthew 16:17-18; John 14:12).

-What can you learn from the way Jesus dealt with sickness, death, and demons to apply in your own ministry?

-What can you learn about the relation of faith and miracles to apply in your ministry?

-What are the results that should follow true miracles of God? How could these results help you distinguish true miracles from deceiving signs of false ministers?

SELF-TEST

1. Write the Key Verses from memory.

_____

_____

_____

2. Define the topical method of Bible study.

_____

_____

_____

3. What are the four steps for doing a topical Bible study?

_____

_____

_____

_____

(Answers to tests are provided at the conclusion of the final chapter in this manual.)

FOR FURTHER STUDY

Continue studying the topic of miracles. Study all the miracles in the book of Matthew.

Create an outline of your study similar to the example given in this chapter. Use the sample chart given in this lesson to analyze each miracle in the book of Matthew. You might also want to complete the study of miracles in the book of Luke which was started in this chapter. Use the chart to analyze each miracle. The New Testament records other miracles in the books of Mark, John, and Acts. You may want to continue to study the topic of miracles in these books.

You may also want to study miracles in the Old Testament. If you do, the following list will help you locate the Old Testament miracles:

Genesis:	1; 19:26
Exodus:	17
Numbers:	6
Joshua:	3
Judges:	3
I and II Samuel:	3
I and II Kings:	26
Daniel:	2
Joel:	1 (Joel 1:17)
Jonah:	1

Sample chart for use in studying miracles:

Miracles In The Book Of: _____						
Miracle	**Realm**	**Occasion**	**People**	**Means**	**Results**	**Reactions**

CHAPTER SEVENTEEN

BIOGRAPHICAL STUDY

OBJECTIVES:

Upon completion of this chapter you will be able to:

- Write the Key Verse from memory.
- Define the biographical study method.
- Do a biographical Bible study.

KEY VERSE:

Now all these things happened unto them for examples; and they are written for our admonition. . . (I Corinthians 10:11)

INTRODUCTION

This chapter defines and explains the biographical method of Bible study, an example of the method is presented, and in the "For Further Study" section you are given the opportunity to do a biographical study.

THE METHOD DEFINED

A biography is the story of someone's life. The biographical method of Bible study focuses on the lives of Bible personalities. By studying the lives of Bible characters you can learn from their experiences. The Bible states:

Now all these things happened unto them for examples; and they are written for our admonition. (I Corinthians 10:11)

Events which happened in the lives of Bible personalities were recorded by the inspiration of the Holy Spirit for your benefit. Their experiences can teach you great spiritual lessons. By observing their failures you can learn of spiritual errors to avoid. By observing their successes you can develop positive spiritual qualities in your own life.

THE METHOD EXPLAINED

STEP ONE: SELECT THE PERSON TO BE STUDIED:

You may choose a personality that is of special interest to you. You might want to choose a person from the list in Hebrews 11, Galatians 3:7 or Luke 4:27. You might study an important person in the Bible book which you are presently reading or studying. Remember that the greatest biographical study of all is the life of Jesus Christ.

Be careful not to confuse names. For example, there are some 30 Zachariahs in the Bible, 20 Nathans, 15 Jonathans, 8 Judases, 7 Marys, 5 James, and 5 Johns. Be sure the verses you study are about the person you have selected and not another individual with the same name.

Also be alert for people who have more than one name. For example, Jacob's name was changed to Israel, Abram's name was changed to Abraham, and Saul's name was changed to the Apostle Paul.

STEP TWO: GATHER THE INFORMATION:

Gather all the information in the Bible on the person you select. If you have a concordance available, look up the name of the person and find a list of all references to him/her in the Bible. If you do not have a concordance, gather the references directly from the Bible. Most of the references concerning a selected Bible personality are found within one book or a series of consecutive books. List all the Bible references about the person you are studying, then look each one up in your Bible and read it.

STEP THREE: ANALYZE THE INFORMATION:

The following list identifies some of the information you should gather and analyze in a biographical study. The Bible may not give information on all of these items in every biography, but try to include everything it does reveal about the person you are studying.

Use the chart found at the conclusion of the "For Further Study" section of this chapter to record and analyze the information you gather.

Biographical information to obtain includes:

Name and meaning of name.
Relatives: Parents, brothers and sisters, ancestors, children.
Birth: Location, importance of birth, unusual events surrounding birth.
Childhood and early training.
Geographical setting: Where does the story of this person's life occur?
Friends and associates, personal relationships.

Occupation or vocation: What position or office did they occupy? How did they earn their living?
Physical description.
Positive character traits.
Negative character traits.
Significant spiritual events:
>First encounter with God
>Conversion
>Call to service
>Greatest crisis or turning point in the person's life: (For example, Saul on the Damascus Road)
Death: When, where, unusual circumstances

STEP FOUR: APPLY WHAT YOU HAVE LEARNED

Make personal applications from the life of the person you have studied. For example:

What were the positive character traits? Ask God to help you develop them in your own life.

What were the negative character traits? Do you see any of these in your own life? Ask God to help you overcome them.

Compose one sentence which summarizes the greatest truth you learned from this life. For example, a statement about the life of Sampson might be "Spiritual compromise results in failure."

EXAMPLE OF THE METHOD

STEP ONE: SELECT THE PERSON TO BE STUDIED:

King Saul

STEP TWO GATHER THE INFORMATION:

The story of Saul is found in I Samuel 9-31. The information on Saul was gathered from these chapters.

STEP THREE: ANALYZE THE INFORMATION:

Name and meaning of name:

Saul. Meaning "Asked of God." I Samuel 9:2

Relatives: Parents, brothers and sisters, ancestors, children:

Son of Kish who was the son of Abiel, the son of Zeror, the son of Bechorath, the son of Aphiah. Kish was a Benjamite and a mighty man of power. I Samuel 9:1

Saul had three sons: Jonathan, Ishui, and Melchishula. He had two daughters: Merab and Michal. His wife's name was Ahinoam. I Samuel 14:49-50

Birth: Location, importance of birth, unusual events surrounding birth.

The Bible does not state these facts.

Childhood and early training:

Cared for his father donkeys: I Samuel 9:3

Geographical Setting:

Judah

Friends and associates, personal relationships:

The children of Belial despised him: I Samuel 10:27. He was close to Abner, the captain of his host, who was his uncle's son: I Samuel 14:50. David became an associate of Saul. At first he was in favor, then Saul became jealous and their relationship was broken: I Samuel 18:6-9. When Saul first became king he had a band of men whose hearts God had touched. When Saul started adding "strong and valiant" men without direction from God, his problems began: I Samuel 10:26; 13:2; 14:52

Occupation or vocation:

First king of Israel.

Physical description:

From his shoulders upward he was higher than any of the people: I Samuel 9:2, 10:23
He was described as "goodly" which means handsome: I Samuel 9:2

Positive character traits:

Showed concern for family	I Samuel 9:5
Choice man	I Samuel 9:2; 10:24
Let spirit change his heart	I Samuel 11:6; 10:6
Modest: Hides among the baggage	I Samuel 10:22
Refuses to execute	I Samuel 11

Leadership: Rallies people	I Samuel 11
Man of the spirit	I Samuel 11
Originally was obedient	I Samuel 9:27
Aligned himself with godly	I Samuel 11:7; 10:26
Bold for God	I Samuel 10:6
Originally was humble	I Samuel 9:21

Negative character traits:

Did what was expedient rather than obeying God: I Samuel 13:8-13

Disobeyed, lied, then refused to accept the blame: I Samuel 15

Grieved God's people: I Samuel 15:35

More concerned with what man thought than God: I Samuel 15:30

Chose strong and valiant men to be close to him rather than the band of men God had touched: I Samuel 10:26; 14:52

Fearful: I Samuel 17:11

Judged by outward appearances: I Samuel 17:33

Trusted the armor of man: I Samuel 17:38

Jealous: I Samuel 18:6-9

Evil spirit: I Samuel 18:10

Spirit of revenge: I Samuel 18:11

Plotted against God's anointed: I Samuel 18:20-30

Significant spiritual events:

First encounter with God:	I Samuel 9:15-27
Conversion:	I Samuel 10:9
Call to service:	I Samuel 10:1
Greatest crisis or turning point:	I Samuel 13

Death: When, where, unusual circumstances:

I Samuel 31: Died by his own hand. His three sons, his armor bearer, and all his men died the same day in Mt. Gilboa during a battle with the Philistines.

STEP FOUR: APPLY WHAT YOU HAVE LEARNED:

Positive character traits in Saul's life which I should seek to develop in my own life:

When the Spirit of the Lord comes on me, I can be changed into "another man": I Samuel 10:6. I should seek that type of anointing from God.

Negative character traits in Saul's life which I should seek to avoid in my own life:

God desires leaders after His own heart: I Samuel 13:14. Although Saul failed in this area, I desire to be such a leader.

Disobedience: Doing what is expedient rather than what God commands. Placing blame on others for my own sin. Caring more what man thinks than what God thinks of me.

I would do well to review the entire list of Saul's negative traits and examine my own heart from time to time.

God's call was for Saul to be captain over the people: I Samuel 10:1. It was people who made him king instead. (I Samuel 12:12-15; 10:24). God was to be Israel's king. I should use caution, lest the praise of people turn me aside from God's plan.

Although God was originally with Saul (I Samuel 10:7, 9; 13:14), He later lost the kingdom. Even after his sin and the prophecy of losing the kingdom, however, God's anointing still rested on Saul (I Samuel 14:47). The gifts and callings of God are without repentance. Saul still heard God's voice (I Samuel 15:1) and worshiped Him (15:31), but he had unconfessed sin and lost the kingdom.

David recognized the danger of touching a man anointed by God as a leader. I should heed this warning.

The greatest truth learned from the life of Saul is the result of disobedience to God. It is summarized in the statement of Samuel: "Behold to obey is better than sacrifice, and to hearken than the fat of rams." I Samuel 15:22

The result of such disobedience is summarized in David's statement about Saul: "How the mighty are fallen." II Samuel 1:19

178

SELF-TEST

1. Write the Key Verse from memory.

_____

_____

_____

2. Define the biographical method of Bible study.

_____

_____

_____

3. List the four steps of the biographical method of Bible study.

_____

_____

_____

_____

(Answers to tests are provided at the conclusion of the final chapter in this manual.)

FOR FURTHER STUDY

Select a Bible character and do a biographical study. Use the following chart for this and other biographical studies you will do in the future.

BIOGRAPHICAL BIBLE STUDY

STEP ONE: SELECT THE PERSON TO BE STUDIED:

STEP TWO: GATHER THE INFORMATION:

List the Bible references which record the life of this person:

STEP THREE: ANALYZE THE INFORMATION:

Name and meaning of name:

Relatives: Parents, brothers and sisters, ancestors, children:

Birth: Location, importance of birth, unusual events surrounding birth:

Childhood and early training:

Geographical setting:

Friends and associates, personal relationships:

Occupation or vocation:

Physical description:

Positive character traits:

Negative character traits:

Significant spiritual events:

    First encounter with God:

    Conversion:

    Call to service:

    Greatest crisis or turning point:

Death:

STEP FOUR: APPLY WHAT YOU HAVE LEARNED:

Positive traits I could develop:

Negative traits I should avoid:

The greatest truth I learned from studying this life is. . .

CHAPTER EIGHTEEN

THE THEOLOGICAL METHOD

OBJECTIVES:

Upon completion of this chapter you will be able to:

- Write the Key Verse from memory.
- Define the theological method of Bible study.
- List five steps of the theological method of Bible study.
- Define the word "doctrine."
- Define key theological terms.
- Do a Bible study using the theological method.

KEY VERSE:

> **Thy testimonies are wonderful: therefore doth my soul keep them.
> (Psalm 119:129)**

INTRODUCTION

This chapter defines and explains the theological method of Bible study. An example of this method is also provided. The "For Further Study" section provides an opportunity to apply what you have learned by actually using the theological method of Bible study.

THE METHOD DEFINED

The theological method focuses on the study of basic Bible doctrines. It is the study of a book or the Bible as a whole in order to collect, compare, and organize doctrine. "Theology" is the study of God. This includes the study of God the Father, Jesus Christ the Son, and the Holy Spirit. The theological method focuses on Bible doctrines that reveal things about God. A doctrine is a group of teachings about a certain subject. The theological method focuses on basic doctrines (collective teachings) of theology (things pertaining to God).

A theological study usually focuses on all a certain book teaches on a selected doctrine. An even more detailed theological study focuses on all the entire Bible teaches on a doctrine. A doctrine is never determined on the basis of one isolated verse or passage. Doctrinal error results from teaching a doctrine based on only a few selected texts. This is a practice followed by false cults.

In doing a theological Bible study you can apply everything you have already learned about book, chapter, paragraph, verse, and word study. All of these study methods can be applied as you use the theological method.

THE METHOD EXPLAINED

There are five major steps in the theological method of Bible study:

STEP ONE: SELECT THE TOPIC

The following outline of Biblical theology will assist you in selecting topics for use in the theological method of Bible study:

Biblical Theology

I.   Bibliology: The study of the doctrine of the Bible.

     A.   Origin
     B.   Revelation
     C.   Inspiration
     D.   Authority
     E.   Illumination (how the Holy Spirit illuminates or helps us understand the Bible)
     F.   Interpretation

II.   Theology: Study of God the Father.

     A.   The attributes of God
     B.   The works of God
     C.   The names of God
     D.   The triune nature of God

III.   Cristology: The study of the doctrine of Jesus Christ.

     A.   The attributes of Jesus
     B.   The works of Jesus
     C.   The names of Jesus
     D.   The triune nature of Jesus
     E.   His life in the flesh:
          1.   Birth and childhood
          2.   Baptism

3.   Temptation
4.   Transfiguration
5.   Teachings
6.   Miracles
7.   Sufferings and death
8.   Resurrection
9.   Ascension

F.   The second return of Jesus Christ
G.   The messianic kingdom
H.   The deity of Jesus: The study of how Jesus was both divine and human, in one person.
I.   His preexistence with God the Father
J.   Old Testament types of Jesus Christ

IV.   Pneumatology: The study of the doctrine of the Holy Spirit.

A.   The attributes of the Holy Spirit
B.   The work and ministry of the Holy Spirit
    1.   In the Old Testament
    2.   In the New Testament
    3.   In the present Church age
C.   The names of the Holy Spirit
D.   Preexistence of the Holy Spirit with God the Father
E.   Triune nature of the Holy Spirit
F.   The Holy Spirit in the Old Testament contrasted with the Holy Spirit in the New Testament
G.   Types and symbols of the Holy Spirit
H.   Gifts of the Holy Spirit
I.   Fruit of the Holy Spirit
J.   Baptism in the Holy Spirit

V.   Angelology: The study of good angels, the angels of God:

A.   Their structure and organization
B.   Names of angels
C.   The work of angels: Past, present, future

VI.   Demonology: The study of wicked angels who are the demons of Satan:

A.   Origin
B.   Structure and organization
C.   Names
D.   Work: Past, present, future

E.   Judgment and destination

VII.   Satanology: Study of Satan:

    A.   Origin
    B.   Fall
    C.   Names
    D.   Work: Past, present, future
    E.   Judgment and destination

VIII.   Anthropology: The study of the origin and nature of man:

    A.   The origin of man
    B.   The fall of man
    C.   The sin nature of man
    D.   God's remedy for man's sin

IX.   Soteriology: The study the doctrine of salvation.

    A.   The development of the plan of Salvation: Traced from the first promise of salvation in Genesis 3:15 throughout the Bible
    B.   Study of the Savior, Jesus Christ (see God the Son Jesus Christ, Cristology)
    C.   The finished work of the Savior
    D.   The terms of salvation

X.   Ecclesiology: This is the study of the doctrine of the Church. It focuses on all the Bible teaches regarding the spiritual Body of Jesus Christ which is called the Church:

    A.   The Church as an organism: The body of Christ
    B.   The contrast between Israel and the Church
    C.   The organization of the Church:
        1.   Ordinances
        2.   Order
        3.   Structure
        4.   Service
        5.   Doctrine of the church

XI.   Eschatology: Study of the last events which are to happen before eternity begins:

    A.   Prophecy concerning the Church
    B.   Prophecy concerning Israel
    C.   Prophecy concerning other nations of the world

D.   Prophecy concerning the Messiah: His returns and establishing of His kingdom

E.   The resurrections of the dead

F.   The judgments

G.   The tribulation

H.   The millennium

I.   The eternal states of the righteous and the unrighteous

STEP TWO: DEFINE THE DOCTRINE SELECTED

The definitions of basic Bible doctrines are given in the preceding outline. These include Cristology, pneumatology, theology, bibliology, angelology, demonology, satanology, anthropology, soteriology, ecclesiology, and eschatology.

STEP THREE: SELECT THE BIBLE PORTION TO BE STUDIED

Decide the book or books of the Bible in which you will study this doctrine. Books of the New Testament are the best to use for theological research. The Old Testament is largely prophetic or in narrative (story) form.   The New Testament, especially the Gospels and the Letters, provide much material for theological Bible study.

STEP FOUR: GATHER INFORMATION ON THE DOCTRINE

Use what you have learned about book, chapter, paragraph, verse, and word studies to help you gather information on the doctrine which you are studying. As you read, make notations on everything the Scriptures reveal about the doctrine.

STEP FIVE: SUMMARIZE THE INFORMATION YOU GATHERED

Summarize the information you recorded during Bible study. Use the outline on theology given in this chapter to help you organize your study notes into an outline or chart.

EXAMPLE OF THE METHOD

STEP ONE: SELECT THE TOPIC

For an example of the theological method we have selected the topic of Cristology.

STEP TWO: DEFINE THE DOCTRINE

Cristology is the study of the doctrines pertaining to Jesus Christ.

STEP THREE: SELECT THE BIBLE PORTION TO BE STUDIED

We will study Cristology in the book of Colossians.

STEP FOUR: GATHER INFORMATION ON THE DOCTRINE

For this study we first read and outlined the book of Colossians:

The Book Of Colossians

I.   Introduction: 1:1-14

      A.   Greetings: 1:1-2
      B.   Thanksgiving: 1:3-8
      C.   Paul's prayer for Christians at Colossae: 1:9-14

II.   The person and work of Jesus: 1:15-23

      A.   Lord of creation: 1:15-17
      B.   Lord of the Church: 1:18-19
      C.   Reconciler: 1:20-23

III.   Paul: God's minister of reconciliation: 1:24-2:7

      A.   Sufferings: 1:24
      B.   Minister of mystery of Christ: 1:25-29
      C.   Desire for unity and stability in Christ: 2:1-7

IV.   Christ's lordship over false teaching: 2:8-3:4

      A.   Lord of every power: 2:8-10
      B.   Source of the new life: 2:11-14
      C.   Conqueror of principalities and power: 2:15
      D.   Colossian practices as denial of Christ's lordship: 2:16-3:4
            1.   Ritual: 2:16-17
            2.   Angel worship: 2:18-19
            3.   Subject to rudiments of world: 2:20-23
            4.   Worldly, temporal affections: 3:1-4

V.   Christ's lordship and the Christian life: 3:5-4:6

      A.   Old life to put off: 3:5-9
      B.   New life to put on: 3:10-17

C.   Special situations: 3:18-4:6
     1.   Home: 3:18-21
     2.   Work: 3:22; 4:1
     3.   General guidelines: 3:23-25

VI. Final instructions: 4:2-6

    A.   Duty of prayer: 4:2-4
    B.   Duty of witness: 4:5-6

VII. Closing: 4:7-18

    A.   Personal greetings: 4:7-17
    B.   Salutation: 4:18

(Note: In addition to outlining the book, you could also do chapter, paragraph, verse, and word studies to study the doctrine within the book. What studies you do depends on how thoroughly you decide to study the subject. For purposes of this example, we have done only an outline on Colossians).

Next, we read the book again and wrote down every reference to Jesus Christ and summarized what was taught by that reference:

Chapter One:

1:1	His name: Jesus Christ.
1:2	Peace comes from Jesus.
1:3	God is Father of the Lord Jesus.
1:4	Faith is in Jesus Christ.
1:13	His Kingdom.
1:14	In Jesus we have redemption and forgiveness of sin.
1:15	Jesus is the image of the invisible God; He is the firstborn of all creation.
1:16	All things were created by Jesus.
1:17	Jesus is before all things and in Him all things consist.
1:18	Jesus is the head of the Church which is His spiritual body.
1:18	Jesus is the firstborn from the dead (this means He was the first to be resurrected from the dead).
1:19	All fullness is in Him.
1:20	Jesus made peace through the blood of His cross.
1:20	Jesus accomplished reconciliation.
1:22	Holiness is through Jesus Christ.
1:24	The Church is His spiritual body.
1:27	When Jesus is within us we have the hope of glory.

1:28	Jesus is our perfection.
1:29	He works in us mightily.

Chapter Two:

2:3	All the treasures of wisdom and knowledge are in Him.
2:5	Jesus is the object of our faith.
2:6	We are to walk in Him.
2:7	We are to grow in Him.
2:9	In Jesus the fullness of the Godhead dwells bodily.
2:10	Jesus is the head of all principalities and powers we are complete in Him.
2:13	Jesus has forgiven us (circumcision of heart).
2:14	Jesus fulfilled all the Old Testament law.
2:15	Jesus judged principalities and powers.
2:17	The body is of Christ.
2:19	He is the head of the body.
2:20	If we are dead with Christ, we are not subject to the rudiments of the world.

Chapter Three:

3:1	We are raised with Jesus.
3:1	He is seated at the right hand of God.
3:4	Jesus is our life.
3:4	Jesus will be manifested and we will be manifested with Him ("manifested" would make a good word study).
3:11	Christ is all and in all; He breaks down walls of separation.
3:10	We are renewed in knowledge after His image
3:13	Forgiveness between brethren is possible on the basis of Christ's forgiveness.
3:15	Peace comes from Jesus.
3:16	His Word is to dwell in us richly.
3:17	We are to do all in His name.
3:17	We are to pray in His name.
3:24	We are to serve the Lord Jesus Christ.

Chapter Four:

4:3	The mystery of Christ (the Gospel).

STEP FIVE: SUMMARIZE THE INFORMATION YOU GATHERED

The following outline analyzes the information gathered in Colossians on Cristology. It summarizes the basic doctrines taught about Jesus in this book:

The Study Of Christology In Colossians

I. The names of Jesus Christ:

    A. Christ Jesus: 1:1
    B. Lord Jesus Christ: 1:3
    C. Head of the Body: 1:18, 24
    D. Son of His love: 1:13
    E. Lord Christ: 3:24

II. The attributes of Jesus Christ:

    A. Omniscient: Knows all (in Him is all wisdom and knowledge): 2:3
    B. Love: He made peace through the blood of His cross because of His love for sinful mankind: 1:20
    C. Holiness: He is perfection: 1:29
    D. Omnipresence: Present everywhere; Christ is in all: 3:11
    E. Infinity: Before all things: 1:17; Christ is all: 3:11
    F. Omnipotent: He is all powerful:
        1. All things are created by Him: 1:16
        2. All is held together by Him: 1:17
        3. Principalities and powers are subject to Him: 2:10
    G. Creator: 1:16
    H. Forgiver: 2:13
    I. Peace: 1:2
    J. Faith: 1:4
    K. Wisdom and knowledge: 2:2-3

III. The Deity of Jesus Christ: He was God in the flesh.

    A. His relationship to God:
        1. Son of God: 1:3, 13
        2. He was made in the image of invisible God: 1:15
        3. In Him dwelt the full Godhead: 1:19; 2:9
    B. His works:
        1. Creator: 1:16
        2. Sustainer of life: 1:17
        3. Savior of mankind: 1:14, 20, 22; 2:13,14
        4. Judged principalities and powers: 2:15
    C. His position:
        1. Head of principalities and powers: 2:10
        2. Object of the believer's faith: 1:4, 2:5
        3. Reason and recipient of believer's service: 3:17

4.   Agent through which a believer approaches God: 3:17
5.   Head of the church, His body: 1:24; 2:17, 19
6.   Head of the Kingdom: 1:13
7.   Seated at the right hand of God: 3:1
8.   He is all and in all: 3:11

IV.   The humanity of Jesus: Although He was God He was also made flesh and lived among man, subject to all the temptations and limitations of man, yet without sin:

A.   He spilt His blood: 1:20
B.   He died: 2:15
C.   He was resurrected from the dead: 2:15; 1:18

V.   His death

A.   Fulfilled the law: 2:17
B.   Brought principalities and powers to judgment: 2:15
C.   Made peace and reconciliation for mankind: 1:20,22
D.   Enabled forgiveness of sins: 2:13; 3:13

VI.   His Resurrection

A.   He was the firstborn or first to rise from the dead: 1:18
B.   He guaranteed our resurrection: 3:1

VII.   His return: He will be manifested in the future and we will be manifested with Him: 3:4

SELF-TEST

1. Several theological terms were defined in this chapter. It is good for you to be familiar with these terms so you will understand them when you hear them used by others or encounter them in Bible study materials.

Look at the terms in List One. Read the definitions in List Two. Select the definition which best describes each term. Write the number of the definition on the blank provided in front of the term which it defines.

List One   **List Two**

_____ Angelology   1. The study of the doctrine of the Bible.

_____ Demonology   2. The study of Jesus Christ.

_____ Soteriology   3. The study of the doctrine of the Church.

_____ Ecclesiology   4. The study of last things.

_____ Eschatology   5. The doctrine of salvation.

_____ Cristology   6. The study of man.

_____ Bibliology   7. The study of good angels.

_____ Anthropology   8. The study of bad angels who are the demons of Satan.

_____ Satanology   9. The study of the doctrine of Satan.

_____ Pneumatology   10. The study of the doctrine of the Holy Spirit.

2. Write the Key Verse from memory.

_____

_____

_____

3. What is the theological method of Bible study?

_____

_____

_____

4. List the five steps of the theological method.

_____

_____

_____

_____

_____

5. Define the word "doctrine."

_____

_____

_____

(Answers to tests are provided at the conclusion of the final chapter in this manual.)

FOR FURTHER STUDY

The doctrine of eschatology is the study of teachings concerning last things. The books of I and II Thessalonians reveal several things about eschatology or last things. They focus specifically on the return of Jesus Christ which is known as the rapture.

The rapture is a future time when Jesus will return in the clouds of Heaven to receive to Himself all true believers. Those believers who have previously died will be resurrected from the dead to meet Him in the air. Believers who are alive on earth will be raptured or raised up to join Jesus and those resurrected from the dead. We will all then dwell forever in the presence of God.

Using the example given in this chapter, do a theological study on the books of I and II Thessalonians. Gather and analyze all the information contained in these books pertaining to eschatology, specifically the return of Jesus Christ.

STEP ONE: SELECT THE TOPIC

STEP TWO; DEFINE THE DOCTRINE

STEP THREE: SELECT THE BIBLE PORTION TO BE STUDIED

STEP FOUR: GATHER INFORMATION ON THE DOCTRINE

STEP FIVE: SUMMARIZE THE INFORMATION YOU HAVE GATHERED

CHAPTER NINETEEN

STUDYING BIBLE POETRY

OBJECTIVES:

Upon completion of this chapter you will be able to:

- Write the Key Verse from memory.
- Identify various forms of Bible poetry.
- Identify various types of Bible poetry.
- Study Bible poetry.

KEY VERSE:

**Seven times a day do I praise thee because of thy righteous judgments.
(Psalm 119:164)**

INTRODUCTION

The Bible is a collection of 66 individual books containing history, drama, romance, adventure, and poetry. The Bible is much more than great literature, but it is great literature both in content and form. When you study the <u>content</u> of a book you study the message of the book. You learn the spiritual truths it reveals.

When you study the <u>form</u> of a book you examine the way a book is organized to present the content. Most of the Bible is in narrative form which presents God's truths in stories which are easy to understand. But five books of the Bible--Job, Psalms, Proverbs, Ecclesiastes, and Song of Solomon--are organized in poetic form. There are additional sections of poetry in other parts of the Bible even though the books are not part of the poetry division. For example, poetry is found in some of the books of law and prophecy.

The poetic form of presenting God's truths is quite different from the narrative (story) form used in most of the Bible. Biblical poetry is also different from most forms of poetry with which you may be acquainted. For these reasons, special guidelines are necessary to help you study these books. This chapter explains the form and types of Bible poetry. This knowledge will help you understand and apply the great spiritual truths found in the poetic books of the Bible.

POETIC FORM

The poetry of the Bible probably will not be like any poetry with which you are familiar. The poetry of the Bible is written in the form of Hebrew poetry since most of the Old Testament was written in this language. The basic principle of Bible poetry is that it contains "parallelism" in thought. The word "parallelism" is from the word "parallel" which means "beside one another or like each other." For example, these two lines are parallel:

When things are parallel to each other, just like these two lines, they are alike. Hebrew poetry is parallel in thought just as these two lines are parallel in appearance. Each line of the poem agrees with other lines of the poem.

There are four common parallel forms used in Hebrew poetry:

1. SYNONYMOUS PARALLELISM:

The word "synonymous" means the same. In synonymous parallel poems the second line of the poem repeats the thought of the first line. For example:

Lord, how are they increased that trouble me!
Many are they that rise up against me. (Psalm 3:1)

He that sitteth in the heavens shall laugh:
The Lord will have them in derision. (Psalm 2:4)

In both of these examples the second line rewords the same thought as the first line. The thought expressed in the second line is synonymous (exactly like) that expressed in the first line.

2. ANTITHETIC PARALLELISM:

"Antithetic" means opposite. In antithetic parallel poems the second line is an opposite thought to the first line. But it is still parallel or like the first line because it is stating a similar truth. It uses an opposite to state a similar truth. This is why it is called antithetic. For example:

For the Lord knoweth the way of the righteous:
But the way of the ungodly shall perish. (Psalm 1:6)

In this example the second line is antithetic (opposite) of the first line. The first line speaks of the way of the righteous. The second tells of the way of the unrighteous. But the second line is still parallel to the first line because it agrees with what is said in the first line by presenting an opposite truth.

3. SYNTHETIC PARALLELISM:

This type of parallelism is like building with blocks. The second line of the poem and all following lines add to or develop the thought of the first line. Study the example below. The second and following lines build on or add to the first line of the poem:

> **Blessed is the man that walketh not in the counsel of the ungodly,**
> **Nor standeth in the way of sinners,**
> **Nor sitteth in the seat of the scornful;**
>
> **But his delight is in the law of the Lord;**
> **And in His law doth he meditate day and night. (Psalm 1:1-2)**

In verse 1, the first line states that a man is blessed if he does not walk in the counsel of the ungodly. The following lines build on this truth by stating that he also should not stand or sit in their way. In verse two the first line tells us this man delights in the law of the Lord. The second line adds to this thought that he meditates in God's law constantly.

4. EMBLEMATIC PARALLELISM:

An "emblem" is something which stands for or illustrates something else. For example, the stars in the flag of the United States of America are emblems of (stand for) the 50 states which are members of the Union. In emblematic parallelism the second and following lines of a poem are an emblem or illustration of the first line. For example:

> **As the hart panteth after the water brooks,**
> **So panteth my soul after thee, O God. (Psalm 42:1)**

The second line of this verse illustrates the first. David pictures his soul desiring God just like a hart (an animal similar to a deer) pants for water when it is thirsty. The illustration of a thirsty deer is an emblem expressing David's spiritual thirst. Although there are several other types of parallel form in Hebrew poetry they are not very common in the Bible so it is not necessary to include them in our study.

USING FORM TO UNDERSTAND CONTENT

Recognizing these basic poetic forms will help you when you study Bible poetry. You will be able to understand the content as it is expressed in:

1. Identical restatements of truth (synonymous parallelism):

This will help you understand the same truth expressed in similar ways. Such repetition will fix the truth expressed firmly in your mind and heart. It is an important way of meditating on the Word

197

of God.   If for some reason you do not understand a certain truth in the way it is presented in the first line of a poem, the following lines which present the same truth will help you understand.

2.   Opposite statements of the same truth (antithetic parallelism):

You will learn not only great truths, but the opposite parallels of these truths.   In the example of Psalms 1:6 you not only learned something about the way of the righteous but you also learned an opposite truth about the way of the ungodly. As you learn to recognize the antithetic parallel form you will be able not only to apply positive truths in your life but you also will be warned of dangers of the opposite.   In the example we used you learned that God knows your way if you are righteous which is a positive truth.   You also learned that if you are unrighteous you will perish. This opposite thought provides an important warning.

3.   Building blocks of truth (synthetic parallelism):

As each line of a poem builds or adds to what is presented in the first line, that truth will be fully developed in your mind.

4.   Emblems which illustrate God's truth (emblematic parallelism):

Such illustrations create a visual picture of God's truths in your mind.

TYPES OF POETRY

There are three basic types of Hebrew poetry.   The division of poetry into types is made on the basis of the content and manner of presentation of the poem.   If you learn to recognize the different types of Bible poetry it will help you understand what you are reading.   The three main types of Bible poetry include:

1.   EPIC POETRY:

This is a narrative poetry.   It tells the story of a heroic action.   There is quite a bit of narrative poetry scattered throughout the books of history.   Read Numbers 22 through 24 which tells the story of Balaam.   It contains examples of epic poetry.

2.   DRAMATIC POETRY:

Dramatic poetry is acted poetry.   The book of Job is the best example of acted poetry.   In the opening we are allowed to see behind the scenes and discover the cause of Job's problems is Satanic.   Next we find messengers informing Job of the disaster of the loss of his children and possessions.   Then Job is sitting by a lonely ash heap. In following scenes his friends offer a variety of suggestions as to the reason why he is suffering.   There is a great climax as Job hears from God and in the end is restored with earthly blessings. The book of Job is a drama presented in poetic form.

3. LYRIC POETRY:

Lyric poetry is sung poetry. Two excellent examples are found in Deborah's song of Judges 5 and Miriam's song in Exodus 15. There are also sections of lyric poetry which were used for mourning or expressing sorrow. Examples of these are found in Psalms 137, 74, 80, and II Samuel 1:19-27. The book of Lamentations is also an example of this type of lyric poetry or mournful singing. This book is written in poetic form but it is classified with the historic books because the poetry relates to a tragic event in the history of God's people.

THE BOOKS OF POETRY: A PROGRESSION

The five books of poetry show a progression of spiritual life. The book of Job describes the death to the old life of self. Psalms shows the new life in God, expressing itself in praise, prayer, adoration, supplication, confession, and intercession. In Proverbs we are in God's school learning heavenly yet practical wisdom for life on earth. Ecclesiastes speaks of the vanity of pursuing life "under the sun" apart from God. The Song of Solomon speaks of the pursuit of life with meaning through a personal relationship with Jesus Christ.

SELF-TEST

1. Write the Key Verse from memory.

_____

_____

2. Look at List One of the types of Biblical poetry. Read List Two and find the definition which describes each type. Write the letter of the correct definition in front of the type of poetry which it describes.

List One

_____Dramatic poetry
_____Epic poetry
_____Lyric poetry

List Two

a. This type of poetry is sung.
b. This type of poetry is a drama.
c. This type of poetry is narrative or in story form and often tells of heroic action.

3. Look at List One of the different forms of Biblical poetry.   Read List Two and find the definition which describes each form. Write the letter of the correct definition in front of the form which it describes.

List One

_____Synonymous parallelism

_____Emblematic parallelism

_____Antithetic parallelism

_____Synthetic parallelism

List Two

a. The second and following lines give an illustration or emblem to express the truth of the first line.
b. The second and following lines opposite truth which relates to the first line of the poem.
c. The second and following lines express a thought identical to the first line.
d. The second and following lines build on the truth expressed in the first line.

4. Look up Psalm 3:1 in your Bible. This verse is written in_____parallelism.
5. Look up Psalm 1:6 in your Bible. This verse is written in_____parallelism.
6. Look up Psalm 1:1-2 in your Bible. This verse is written in _____parallelism.
7. Look up Psalm 42:1 in your Bible. This verse is written in_____parallelism.

(Answers to tests are provided at the conclusion of the final chapter in this manual.)

FOR FURTHER STUDY

In addition to the books of poetry there are scattered poetical sections in both the Old and New Testaments. Some of these are listed below. Use these references for further study of Bible poetry:

Genesis 4:23-24	Lamech to his wives
Exodus 15:1-21	Song of Moses/Miriam
Numbers 21:27-30	Song of ballad singers
Numbers 23:7-10	Song of Balaam
Deuteronomy 33:1-47	Song of Moses
Joshua 10:12-14	Song of Joshua
Judges 5:1-31	Song of Deborah and Barak
Ruth 1:16-17	Song of Ruth
I Samuel 2:1-10	Song of Hannah
II Samuel 3:33-34	David's lament for Abner
II Samuel 1:17-27	Song for Saul and Jonathan
II Samuel 22:2-51	David's song of victory
II Samuel 23:1-7	David's last words
I Chronicles 16:8-36	David's thanksgiving
Jeremiah 9:17-22	Mourning over the fallen nation
Lamentations 1,2,3,4,5	Mourning over the fallen nation
Ezekiel 27:25-28:23	Prophecies against Tyre, poetic form
Ezekiel 19:1-14	Lamentation for Israel's princes
Hosea 2:1-15	Song of the chastisement of Israel
Habakkuk 3:1-19	Habakkuk's prayer
Luke 1:46-55	Mary's song
Luke 1:68-79	Song of Zacharias
Luke 2:29-32	Simeon's blessing

CHAPTER TWENTY

STUDYING BIBLE PROPHECY

OBJECTIVES:

Upon completion of this chapter you will be able to:

- Write the Key Verse from memory.
- List three reasons why it is important to study Bible prophecy.
- Identify the source of Biblical prophecy.
- Define Biblical prophecy.
- Name two methods by which God gave prophecies.
- Distinguish between true and false prophets.
- List three purposes of prophecy.
- List five keys for understanding Biblical prophecy.

KEY VERSE:

And He said unto them, These are the words which I spake unto you, while I was yet with you, that all things must be fulfilled, which were written in the law of Moses, and in the prophets, and in the Psalms concerning me. (Luke 24:44)

INTRODUCTION

As you learned previously in this course, there are several books in God's Word which are called books of prophecy. This chapter presents basic guidelines for studying and understanding Bible prophecy.

A BOOK OF PROPHECY

God's written Word, the Holy Bible, differs in many ways from the sacred writings of other religions. But there is one important difference. That difference is that the sacred books of all other religions, but do not contain prophecies that have been accurately fulfilled. The prophecy contained in the Bible, much of which has already been fulfilled, is an important witness of the divine inspiration of the Scriptures.

DEFINITION OF PROPHECY

The word "prophecy" means to speak forth. Bible prophecy includes three basic kinds of speaking forth:

1. A message of inspiration from God.
2. Prediction of future events in God's eternal plan.
3. An interpretation for man of the acts of God.

THE PROPHETS

God commissioned each prophet of the Bible to fulfill a particular role in His plan.

-As <u>interpreters</u> they explained God's acts to men.

-As <u>spokesmen</u> they voiced God's truth. They spoke messages of hope and inspiration.

-As <u>prophets</u> they predicted future events in God's plan through revelation given by the Holy Spirit.

The predictions of Bible prophecy are beyond the power of human ability. They include a sufficient number of details to eliminate speculation or guessing.

METHODS OF PROPHECY

There are two basic ways in which God spoke through the prophets.

THE SPOKEN WORD:

The method most often used was the spoken word. God would tell the prophet the words to speak. For example, God said to the prophet Jeremiah:

> **. . . for thou shalt go to all that I shall send thee, and whatsoever I command thee thou shalt speak. (Jeremiah 1:7)**

Throughout the book of Jeremiah God's instructions to him were. . .

> **Go and cry in the ears of Jerusalem, saying, Thus saith the Lord. . . (Jeremiah 2:2)**

Jeremiah spoke the words which God told him to speak.

ACTED PROPHECIES:

In addition to spoken prophecy, God had the prophets visually act out a message. For example, God told Jeremiah to:

> . . . Make thee bonds and yokes and put them upon thy neck. . .
> (Jeremiah 27:2)

These yokes were a visual prophecy of the yokes of bondage which were to come on the people because of their sin. Jeremiah acted out the prophetic message of God.

THE SOURCE OF PROPHECY

The source of Biblical prophecy is God who reveals His message to man through the Holy Spirit:

> For the prophecy came not in old time by the will of man; but holy men of God spake as they were moved by the Holy Ghost. (II Peter 1:21)

> But God hath revealed them unto us by His Spirit: for the Spirit searcheth all things, yea, the deep things of God.   (I Corinthians 2:10)

God can speak accurately of the future because:

> Known unto God are all His works from the beginning of the world.
> (Acts 15:18)

> Remember the former things of old: for I am God, and there is none else; I am God, and there is none like me.

> Declaring the end from the beginning, and from ancient times the things that are not yet done, saying, My counsel shall stand, and I will do all my pleasure.
> (Isaiah 46:9-10)

God raises up true prophets:

> The Lord thy God will raise up unto thee a Prophet from the midst of thee, of thy brethren, like unto me; unto him ye shall hearken.   (Deuteronomy 18:15)

God reveals His future plans to these prophets:

> Surely the Lord God will do nothing but He revealeth His secret unto His servants the prophets. (Amos 3:7)

FALSE PROPHETS

Satan imitates true prophecy through false predictions by fortune tellers, witches, and astrologers. These methods are not of God. The Prophet Daniel said:

> **Daniel answered in the presence of the king and said, The secret which the king hath demanded cannot the wise men, the astrologers, the magicians, the soothsayers shew unto the king.**

> **But there is a God in heaven that revealeth secrets and maketh known to the king Nebuchadnezzar what shall be in the latter days. . .**
> **(Daniel 2:27-28)**

True prophecy directs attention to Jesus Christ:

> **Wherefore I give you to understand, that no man speaking by the Spirit of God calleth Jesus accursed; and that no man can say that Jesus is the Lord, but by the Holy Ghost. (I Corinthians 12:3)**

The Bible warns of false prophets (Matthew 24:11,24; Mark 13:22). A person called "the false prophet" will be evident in events at the end of the world (Revelation 13:11-17; 16:13; 19:20; 20:10). The Bible reveals several ways to identify false prophets:

-They teach sexual immorality and permissiveness: II Peter 2:13

-They try to lead people away from obedience to God's Word: Deuteronomy 13:1-5

-They make false claims: Matthew 24:23-24

-They deceive people with miraculous signs: Matthew 24:11,24

-They do not prophecy according to the proportion of faith (in right relation to God's Word): Romans 12:6

-False prophets do not have the fruit of the Holy Spirit in their lives: Matthew 7:15-16; Galatians 5:22-23

-What they prophesy does not come to pass: Deuteronomy 18:20-22

THE PURPOSES OF PROPHECY

The Bible reveals special purposes for God speaking to men through prophecy:

TO AUTHENTICATE GOD'S MESSAGE:

Fulfilled prophecy proves that God's message is authentic (true). In Isaiah 41:21-23 God challenges the gods of the heathen nations to prove their power by foretelling future events. They could not do it because they were false gods:

> **Produce your cause, saith the Lord; bring forth your strong reasons, saith the King of Jacob.**
>
> **Let them bring them forth, and shew us what shall happen: let them shew the former things, what they be, that we may consider them, and known the latter end of them; or declare us things for to come.**
>
> **Shew the things that are to come hereafter, that we may know that ye are gods. (Isaiah 41:21-23)**

TO CONFIRM GOD'S MESSENGER:

Prophecy confirms the true messengers of God:

> **The prophet which prophesieth of peace, when the word of the prophet shall come to pass, then shall the prophet be known, that the Lord hath truly sent him. (Jeremiah 28:9)**

TO INSTRUCT BELIEVERS:

Believers are to receive instruction from prophecy and take heed (pay attention) to it:

> **We have also a more sure word of prophecy; whereunto ye do well that ye take heed, as unto a light that shineth in a dark place. . . (II Peter 1:19)**

IMPORTANCE OF STUDYING PROPHECY

There are three main reasons why it is important to study Bible prophecy:

1. All Scripture is inspired of God and is profitable for study:

> **All Scripture is given by inspiration of God, and is profitable for doctrine, for reproof, for correction, for instruction in righteousness;**
>
> **That the man of God may be perfect, thoroughly furnished unto all good works. (II Timothy 3:16-17)**

2. Prophecy brings understanding of past, present, and future events in the plan of God:

> **. . . the things which thou hast seen, and the things which are, and the things which shall be hereafter. (Revelation 1:19)**

3. Understanding of God's future plan prevents deception by Satan:

> **Then if any man shall say unto you, Lo, here is Christ, or there; believe it not.**
>
> **For there shall arise false Christs, and false prophets, and shall shew great signs and wonders: insomuch that, if it were possible, they shall deceive the very elect. BEHOLD, I HAVE TOLD YOU BEFORE.**
>
> **Wherefore if they shall say unto you, behold He is in the desert; go not forth: behold He is in the secret chambers; believe it not. (Matthew 24:23-26)**

God's future plan has been shared before it happens so we will not be deceived by Satan.

4. There is a special blessing pronounced upon those who study Bible prophecy:

> **Blessed is he that readeth, and they that hear the words of this prophecy, and keep those things which are written therein: for the time is at hand. (Revelation 1:3)**

THE STUDY OF PROPHECY

Bible prophecy is part of the "meat" of the Word of God which we referred to previously in this course. The "meat" of prophecy is more difficult to understand than the "milk" of God's Word which presents basic concepts of the Christian faith.

If you are a new believer and do not have any background knowledge of the Bible, you should study other portions of God's Word before you try to study the prophetic books. Study the Gospels, Acts, and Letters of the New Testament. Study the Poetry, Law, and History divisions of the Old Testament. As you study, use what you have learned in this course about book, chapter, paragraph, verse, and word study.

After you have a basic knowledge of these divisions, then study the prophetic books of the Bible. Do not worry if you do not understand all of the prophecies in the Bible. Many great Bible scholars have debated for years about the meaning of some portions of Bible prophecy.

PROPHETIC BOOKS

In addition to the books of prophecy there are many other chapters and verses of prophecy scattered throughout God's Word.

The very first prophecy recorded in the Bible is in the book of Genesis:

> **And I will put enmity between thee and the woman, and between thy seed and her seed: it shall bruise thy head, and thou shalt bruise His heel. (Genesis 3:15)**

This verse prophesies the coming of Jesus Christ who, through His death for the sins of man, would crush the enemy, Satan.

It is not possible to list in this manual every prophecy in the Word of God. We just want you to be aware that there are prophecies throughout the entire Bible. Prophecy is not just confined to the books known as the Books of Prophecy. With study and experience you will be able to identify the prophetic theme that runs throughout the entire Bible.

UNDERSTANDING PROPHECY

Some people are frustrated when they try to study Bible prophecy. Because prophecy is more difficult than other portions of the Bible, they wonder if God really intended for them to understand it. It _is_ possible to understand Bible prophecy. God wanted so much for Daniel to understand prophecy that he sent an angel to explain it to him. The angel said:

> **. . . I am now come forth to give thee skill and understanding. (Daniel 9:22)**

Jesus took time to explain Old Testament prophecy to His Disciples:

> **And He said unto them, These are the words which I spake unto you, while I was yet with you, that all things must be fulfilled, which were written in the law of Moses, and in the prophets, and in the psalms concerning me. (Luke 24:44)**

When the Disciples asked Jesus about the end of the world, Jesus listed several prophetic signs for which they were to watch. He wanted them to understand future events. Jesus said:

> **So likewise ye, when ye shall see all these things, know that it is near, even at the doors. (Matthew 24:33)**

In the introduction to the book of Revelation, a book which some consider quite difficult to understand, it is clear that God wants His people to understand prophecy:

The Revelation of Jesus Christ which God gave unto Him, to shew unto His servants things which must shortly come to pass. . . (Revelation 1:1)

KEYS TO UNDERSTANDING

There are some basic keys which will help you understand and properly interpret Bible prophecy.

ONE: THE BASIC THEME OF PROPHECY

The Lord Jesus Christ is the basic theme of Bible prophecy. There are many other subjects of Bible prophecy. For example, there are prophecies of judgment of wicked nations by God. But the underlying theme of all Bible prophecies is that they somehow relate to Jesus and the purpose of God regarding Him:

Having made known unto us the mystery of His will, according to His good pleasure which He hath purposed in Himself;

That in the dispensation of the fullness of times He might gather together in one all things in Christ, both which are in heaven, and which are on earth; even in Him. (Ephesians 1:9-10)

All Bible prophecy, even when it deals with subjects such as judgment upon nations, etc., relates to the overall plan of God. That plan is to bring all mankind into right relationship with God through the Lord Jesus Christ. The purpose is to gather in one all things in Christ.

The Bible states that the "spirit" or theme of Bible prophecy is Jesus:

. . . for the testimony of Jesus is the spirit of prophecy. (Revelation 19:10)

When you study Bible prophecy consider it in terms of this question: How does this prophecy relate to Jesus Christ (the spirit of prophecy) and God's overall plan concerning Him?

TWO: THE BIBLE INTERPRETS ITSELF

Another key to understanding is to realize that often the Bible explains its own prophecies. For an example of how the Bible interprets itself read Daniel chapter 2. Here a king by the name of Nebuchadnezzar is given a dream from God. Upon waking he cannot remember the dream. He calls upon the astrologers and magicians to recall and interpret the dream. They cannot do it. Then God uses the prophet Daniel to tell the king what he dreamed and interpret it for him. The dream is described by Daniel in verses 31-35. The interpretation of the dream is given in verses 36- 45. This is an example of how, in many passages, the Bible interprets its own prophecies.

The New Testament interprets many of the prophecies of the Old Testament because much of the Old Testament is fulfilled in the New Testament. For example, compare this Old Testament prophecy and the New Testament fulfillment:

> . . . and I will say to them which were not my people, Thou art my people, and they shall say, Thou art my God. (Hosea 2:23)

> Even us, whom He hath called, not of the Jews only, but also of the Gentiles?

> As he saith also in Osee, I will call them my people, which were not my people; and her beloved, which was not beloved.

> And it shall come to pass that in the place where it was said unto them, ye are not my people; there shall they be called the children of the living God. (Romans 9:24-26)

Fulfilled prophecy in the New Testament includes many Old Testament prophecies concerning the coming Messiah, Jesus Christ.

THREE: THE RULE OF DOUBLE REFERENCE

Another key to understanding Bible prophecy is the "rule of double reference." This rule for interpreting Bible prophecy states that a prophecy of immediate fulfillment is made as a means of teaching a deeper truth or foretelling an event to be fulfilled farther in the future.

Many times in the Bible a prophecy was fulfilled immediately after it was given, but the same prophecy applied not only to the event which was fulfilled immediately, but also to a second fulfillment farther in the future.

For example, there is a prophecy given in Ezekiel 28:1-19 which is addressed to Ethbaal who was then the king of Tyre. He was a wicked king. He was a type of the Antichrist who will arise during the end of the world. By saying Ethbaal is a "type" we mean that in nature and actions he was like the Antichrist which will come in the future. (You will learn more about "types" in the next chapter.) When God spoke in prophecy through Ezekiel, it was fulfilled in the immediate future in the life of Ethbaal. But there is a future event, as yet unfulfilled, where the same prophecy applies to the evil end time ruler called the Antichrist.

As you study Bible prophecy remember this rule of double reference. Ask yourself two questions:

1. What did this prophecy mean at the time it was given for the people to whom it was given?
2. Is there a future double reference in this prophecy?

Asking these questions will help you interpret prophecy to the full extent of its meaning.

FOUR: PROPHETIC PERSPECTIVE

The prophets described future events as if they were continuous and in immediate order. For example, Isaiah prophesied:

> **The Spirit of the Lord God is upon me; because the Lord hath anointed me to preach good tidings unto the meek; He hath sent me to bind up the broken hearted, to proclaim liberty to the captives, and the opening of the prison to them that are bound;**

> **To proclaim the acceptable year of the Lord, and the day of vengeance of our God; to comfort all that mourn;**

> **To appoint unto them that mourn in Zion, to give unto them beauty for ashes, the oil of joy for mourning, the garment of praise for the spirit of heaviness; that they might be called trees of righteousness, the planting of the Lord, that He might be glorified. (Isaiah 61:1-3)**

When Jesus read from this portion of Isaiah in Luke 4:17-20 He stopped with the phrase "to proclaim the acceptable year of the Lord." Then He closed the book and said that these Scriptures were fulfilled in Him that day. By this He meant that He was fulfilling this prophecy. He was the one with God's Spirit upon Him to preach good tidings, bind up the broken hearted, proclaim liberty, and open the prisons.

But it is significant that Jesus stopped reading with the phrase "to proclaim the acceptable year of the Lord." He did not read the portion regarding "the day of vengeance of our God" because the day of vengeance had not yet come. Already a gap of almost 2,000 years has elapsed since Jesus read this passage. The day of God's vengeance still has not yet come.

Prophetic perspective records events as if they were immediate. Through the revelation of the Holy Spirit Isaiah saw the whole plan of God. He saw Jesus coming to preach, bind up, proclaim liberty, open the prison, proclaim the acceptable year of the Lord, and bring the vengeance of God.

Isaiah saw the events as you would look at distant ranges of mountains. The valleys in between the mountains are not visible until you climb to the top of the nearest range. Prophetic perspective reveals the whole plan of God from a distance. Sometimes events seem to appear as though they happen immediately in sequence. But as the prophecies are fulfilled there are often valleys of time between them as illustrated by this passage from Isaiah. Jesus has not yet fulfilled the Scriptures about the day of vengeance.

FIVE: THE CONDITIONAL NATURE OF PROPHECY

Much Bible prophecy is conditional in nature. This means that God says He will do certain things based on the response of man. IF man does NOT listen to God's message, certain things will happen. IF man HEARS God's message and RESPONDS properly to it, then something else will happen.

God said:

> **At what instant I shall speak concerning a nation, and concerning a kingdom, to pluck up, and to pull down, and to destroy it;**
>
> **IF that nation, against whom I have pronounced, turn from their evil, I will repent of the evil that I thought to do unto them.**
>
> **And at what instant I shall speak concerning a nation, and concerning a kingdom, to build and to plant it,**
>
> **IF it do evil in my sight, that it obey not my voice, then I will repent of the good, wherewith I said I would benefit them. (Jeremiah 18:7-10)**

In much Bible prophecy, you must continue studying in order to discover man's response to it because the fulfillment of prophecy is often conditional upon man's response. For a good example of this principle read the book of Jonah. The Prophet Jonah revealed that God would destroy Ninevah in three days IF they did not repent. The destruction never came. The reason was that Ninevah responded properly to the message of God and repented of their sins.

OLD TESTAMENT PROPHECY

Prophecy in the Old Testament centers on:

1. Prophecy to the people of Israel which was the nation God raised up through which to reveal Himself to the world. During the period of time when Israel was divided into two kingdoms this prophecy is directed to Israel and Judah. An example of prophecy to Israel is the book of Hosea. An example of prophecy to Judah is the book of Joel.

2. Prophecies to the nations surrounding the people of Israel. For example, prophecies are given regarding Babylon, Egypt, Tyre, Edom, etc. An example is the prophecy of Obadiah directed to the nation of Edom.

3. Prophecies concerning the coming Messiah, Jesus Christ. These are not contained in any one prophetic book. They are scattered throughout the Old Testament. A good example is Isaiah 7:14.

4. Prophecies concerning the entire world, its destiny, future events, the end of the world, and the end of time as we know it. The book of Daniel is an excellent example of this type of prophecy. The following chart condenses the general content of the books of prophecy in the Old Testament. As you use this chart be sure to remember the rule of double reference. Although prophecies were directed to certain nations and fulfilled in the immediate future, many of the prophecies spoke of even greater events in the far future:

Old Testament Prophets

Prophet	Message	Time Period
Jonah Nahum	God loves the Gentiles Doom of Ninevah for its brutality	To Assyria Before Captivity (800-650 B.C.)
Obadiah	Doom of Edom for its treachery	To Edom Before Captivity (800 B.C.)
Hosea Amos	God's love for adulterous Israel God's people ripe for punishment	To Israel Before Captivity (750 B.C.)
Isaiah Jeremiah/ Lamentations Joel Micah Habakkuk Zephaniah	Messiah is coming Judgment now, glory to follow Judgment will fall like a plague God's people on trial The just shall live by faith God's day is coming	To Judah Before Captivity (800-606 B.C.)
Ezekiel Daniel	God is not finished with Israel God's hand in world events	To Judah During Captivity (606-536 B.C.)
Haggai Zechariah Malachi	The danger of halfheartedness The glory of Messiah The danger of hardheartedness	To Judah After Captivity (536-400 B.C.)

NEW TESTAMENT PROPHECY

There are many prophecies scattered throughout the New Testament. Most of these deal with future events which are to happen prior to the end of the world. For examples read the prophecies in Matthew chapter 24.

There is only one book in the prophecy division in the New Testament, however. That is the book of Revelation. John, a Disciple of Jesus, was given this revelation from God through the Holy Spirit. It is a revelation of Jesus Christ:

> **The Revelation of Jesus Christ, which God gave unto him, to shew unto his servants things which must shortly come to pass. . . (Revelation 1:1)**

John was told to. . .

> **Write the things which thou hast seen, and the things which are, and the things which shall be hereafter. (Revelation 1:19)**

The Book of Daniel should be studied along with the book of Revelation as the two books relate to each other.

There are many different interpretations given to the prophecies in the book of Revelation. Most of these interpretations center on the exact timing of certain events or specific details of these events. It is important to have a general understanding, however, of what the Bible says will happen. The following outline provides understanding of the major events:

MAJOR EVENTS IN THE FUTURE

I.   The Bible teaches that Jesus will return to earth for believers: John 14:2-3.

     A.   The Rapture: I Thessalonians 4:13-18 gives the most detail about Christ's return for believers. This return is called the rapture:
          1.   Christ Himself will return: Verse 16
          2.   There will be a resurrection from the grave of those who were believers when they died: Verse 16
          3.   There will be rapture, which means "the act of taking a person from one place to another." Living believers will be taken from earth to meet Jesus: Verse 17.
          4.   There will be a reunion between believers who have previously died, believers living at the time of Christ's return, and the Lord Jesus Christ: Verse 17.

B.   The Tribulation: The Bible tells of a terrible time on earth which is called the tribulation.

　　　1.   The tribulation will last for 42 months or 1,260 days: Daniel 9:24-27
　　　2.   It will be a very difficult time. There have been many difficult times in the world, but three things will distinguish the tribulation from all other times of trouble.
　　　　　a.   First, it will be worldwide and not just local: Revelation 3:10
　　　　　b.   Second, people will realize the end of the world is near: Revelation 6:16
　　　　　c.   Third, the intensity of the trouble will be greater than ever before experienced: Matthew 24:4-14
　　　3.   Its description: There are a series of judgments on earth during the tribulation. These are described in Revelation chapters 6, 8-9, and 16 and Matthew 24:4-14.
　　　4.   The reason for the tribulation: The wickedness of man must be punished, Satan defeated, and Jesus acknowledged as Lord of all. This completes God's plan of the ages spoken of in Ephesians 1:8-9.

C.   The timing of the rapture: Some people believe the rapture will occur before the tribulation and that believers will not have to experience any of this terrible time on earth. Others believe the rapture will happen midway through this period. Still other believe the rapture will happen at the end of the tribulation. The most common interpretation is that the rapture of believers will happen before the tribulation begins. The different views of the timing of the rapture result from various interpretations of prophetic information given in Revelation and other books of the Bible. What is most important is to know you are a true believer and will be ready to go with Jesus in the rapture when it does occur.

D.   The Millennium: The Millennium is a period of 1,000 years after the tribulation during which Jesus will rule the earth in righteousness (Zechariah 14:9; Daniel 7:14). The city of Jerusalem will be the center of government (Isaiah 2:3). This period will end when Satan stages a last revolt against God (Revelation 20:7-9). God will send fire from heaven and end all opposition. Satan will be cast into the lake of fire for eternity. (Revelation 20:10).

E.   Judgment: All created beings will be judged by God. This is known as the time of eternal judgment. Those who died as unbelievers will be resurrected to face judgment. Because they did not repent from sin and accept Jesus as Savior they will be condemned to eternity in Hell (Revelation 20:12-15). True believers who repented from sin and accepted Jesus as Savior will spend eternity in heaven in the presence of God (Revelation 21).

SELF-TEST

1. Write the Key Verse from memory.

_____

_____

_____

_____

2. List three purposes of Biblical prophecy.

_____

_____

_____

3. List four reasons why it is important to study prophecy.

_____

_____

_____

4. List five keys to understanding Bible prophecy.

_____

_____

_____

_____

5. Who is the source of Bible prophecy?

_____

6. Define the word "prophecy."

_____

_____

7. Identify the three kinds of "speaking forth" involved in Biblical prophecy.

_____

_____

_____

8. What two methods did God use in the Bible to give a prophetic message to men?

_____

_____

9. Where is the first prophecy in the Bible found?

_____

10. The Bible gives several ways to identify false prophets. List at least three of these.

_____

_____

_____

(Answers to tests are provided at the conclusion of the final chapter in this manual.)

FOR FURTHER STUDY

1. Apply what you have learned in this lesson to study of the following prophetic books:

Old Testament:

___Isaiah ___Jeremiah ___Lamentations ___Ezekiel ___Daniel ___Hosea ___ Joel

___Amos ___Obadiah ___Jonah ___Micah ___Nahum ___Habakkuk ___Zephaniah

___ Haggai ___Zechariah ___Malachi

New Testament:

___Revelation

2. God speaks through prophecy in the Bible to His people. He also uses prophets in the church to speak to His people:

> **And God hath set some in the church, first apostles, secondarily prophets. . .**
> **(I Corinthians 12:28)**

The messages given by prophets today do not become part of the written Word of God. Their messages are given in confirmation of the written Word of God. What they say is to be judged by its accuracy in relation to the Bible.

For further study of the gift of prophecy as it operates in the church today obtain the Harvestime International Institute course entitled *"Ministry of the Holy Spirit."* This course presents a more detailed discussion of this spiritual gift and lists references on all the prophets of the Bible for further study.

CHAPTER TWENTY-ONE

THE TYPOLOGICAL METHOD

OBJECTIVES:

Upon completion of this chapter you will be able to:

- Write the Key Verse from memory.
- Define the typological method.
- List four general groups into which all Bible types are classified.
- Do a typological Bible study.

KEY VERSE:

> **For the law having a shadow of good things to come, and not the very image of the things, can never with those sacrifices which they offered year by year continually make the comers thereunto perfect. (Hebrews 10:1)**

INTRODUCTION

This chapter explains how to study the Bible by the typological method. This method is also referred to as study by "types." The method is defined, explained, and an example is provided. In the "For Further Study" section you are given an opportunity to do a topological Bible study.

THE METHOD DEFINED

To understand how to do a typological study you must first understand the meaning of the word type. There are several verses in the Bible which explain the meaning of a Biblical type. The Key Verse for this chapter, Hebrews 10:1, speaks of the law having a shadow of good thing to come. "Shadow" is one word to describe a Biblical type. A shadow is an exact outline, although the details may be dim and sometimes it contrasts the thing that casts the shadow.

"Figure" is another word which describes type:

Nevertheless death reigned from Adam to Moses, even over them that had not sinned after the similitude of Adam's transgression, who is the figure of Him that was to come. (Romans 5:14)

According to this verse, Adam was a "figure" of someone else who was to come. The meaning of the word "figure" is similar to that of type. Adam was a type of the Lord Jesus Christ who was to come later.

The offering of sacrifices for sin in the Old Testament was a type of the final sacrifice for sin which was to be offered by Jesus in the New Testament:

The Holy Ghost thus signifying that the way into the holiest of all was not yet made manifest, while as the first tabernacle was yet standing:

Which was a figure for the time then present, in which were offered both gifts and sacrifices that could not make him that did the service perfect, as pertaining to the conscience. (Hebrews 9:8-9)

"Pattern" is another word describing Biblical types:

For if he were on earth, he should not be a priest, seeing that there are priests that offer gifts according to the law;

Who serve unto the example and shadow of heavenly things, as Moses was admonished of God when he was about to make the tabernacle: for, See, saith he, that thou make all things according to the pattern shewed to thee in the mount. (Hebrews 8:4-5)

Each of these words--shadow, figure, and pattern--all contain the idea we refer to when we speak of types. A type is a person or thing in the Bible which God used to represent some other person, thing, or event that would appear in the future. It was a shadow, a figure, or a pattern of what was to come.

THE METHOD EXPLAINED

When we study these types it is called typological Bible study. We study a person, place, event, or thing and then we study the thing of which it is a type. In a way, types are like prophecy. They give an advance view of what is to come in God's future plan. Like prophecy, some types have been fulfilled. Others remain to be fulfilled.

Although the type is important in itself, it has an even greater significance in the future person or event which it represented. Types are physical pictures of spiritual realities. For example, the experience of the children of Israel being healed from the bites of serpents is an actual Old

Testament event. The Old Testament account in Numbers 21:6-9 tells that serpents bit the people and caused many of them to die. Moses made a bronze serpent and set it on a pole. Everyone who looked at the bronze serpent recovered from the serpent's bite. This event is a type of the death of Jesus:

> **And as Moses lifted up the serpent in the wilderness, even so must the Son of man be lifted up; that whosoever believeth in Him should not perish, but have eternal life. (John 3:14-15)**

Many of the truths of the Bible are so simply stated that a child can understand them. There are other truths that are "hidden riches of secret places." They require more intense study to understand. The typical teachings of the Bible are like hidden riches. You must take time to search out these truths to discover the richest teachings of the Word of God.

All types fall into four general classifications:

1. Persons
2. Places
3. Events (historical, ceremonial, etc.)
4. Material things

EXAMPLE OF THE METHOD

One of the greatest types in the Bible is found in the Old Testament personality of Joseph. Read the story of Joseph in Genesis chapters 37-50. Joseph was a type of the Lord Jesus Christ. There were many events in his life which were a pattern of those which would be in the life of Jesus. These are noted on the following chart:

Typological Bible Study

STUDY OF JOSEPH	as a type of	JESUS CHRIST
Reference	**Event**	**References**

Reference	Event	References
Genesis 37:2	He was a shepherd	John 10:11
Genesis 37:3	He was the well-beloved of his father	
Genesis 37:4	He was hated by his own brothers	
Genesis 37:8	His brothers rejected his rulership	
Genesis 37:11	His father took notice of the future plans just as Mary did concerning Jesus	
Genesis 37:13	His father sent him to his brothers	
Genesis 37:13	He was willing to do his father's will	
Genesis 37:18	His brothers plotted against him	
Genesis 37:29	As in the case of Pilate and Jesus, a leader (Reuben) tried to find a way to deliver him	
Genesis 37:23	He was stripped of his beautiful robe	
Genesis 37:28	He was sold for silver	
Genesis 37:26-28	He was sold by Judah (Judas in Greek)	
Genesis 39:2	He became a servant	
Genesis 39:7-23	He resisted temptation	
Genesis 39:13-20	He was condemned by false witnesses	
Genesis 39:20	He suffered though innocent	
Genesis 40:1-3	He was with two sinners in his suffering: One delivered and one was not	
Genesis 41:14	He came up out of the "grave" of prison	
Genesis 41:57	He saved the world from death	
Genesis 47:1-2	His brothers gained access to the king through him	
Genesis 41:50	He had a Gentile bride	
Genesis 50:14-21	He showed a forgiving spirit	

Joseph's life was important in itself but it was also a pattern of an even greater life which was to come in the future. That greater life was the life of the Lord Jesus Christ. You will notice on the chart that space is provided for references under the column heading "Jesus Christ." Complete the typological study by finding references in the Gospels which tell of similar events in the life of Jesus. The first one is done as an example for you to follow. This is an example of typological Bible study, Joseph being a type of Jesus Christ. After you complete the "Self-Test," use the "For Further Study" section of this chapter to do your own typological study.

SELF-TEST

1. Write the Key Verse from memory.

_____

_____

_____

_____

2. Define the typological method of Bible study.

_____

_____

3. What are some other words used in the Bible for the word "types"?

_____

4. What are the four general categories into which Bible types are classified?

_____

_____

_____

_____

5. What Old Testament personality was used in this chapter as an example of a Bible type?

_____

6. Of whom was he a type?

_____

(Answers to tests are provided at the conclusion of the final chapter in this manual.)

FOR FURTHER STUDY

Several examples of types are given in this section which you may use to do a typological Bible study. There is a study form at the end of this section to use in doing typological studies.

1. Study Isaac as a type of Jesus Christ. (Genesis 21-28)

Some things to watch for: Isaac was an only begotten son and he was willing to be sacrificed on a mountain. He also chose a bride, Rebekah.

2. Study Rebekah as a type of the church which is the bride of Christ. (Genesis 24)

She had to be qualified by belonging to the family of Abraham, she had to make her own choice as to whether to come to Isaac, and she had to leave her former surroundings. After her long journey she saw Isaac face to face.

3. Study Noah's ark as a type of salvation. (Genesis 6-8).

Note that the penalty of sin was death. The flood is a type of the judgment of God. The provision of safety in the ark was planned exactly, there was only one door, and there was adequate room for all. The ark was covered with pitch to keep out the water. The word "pitch" comes from a Hebrew word meaning "to cover." The same word is translated "atonement" in other portions of the Old Testament. How is this a type of salvation through Jesus Christ?

4. Study the wanderings of Israel recorded in Exodus, Numbers and Deuteronomy.

I Corinthians 10:11 states that ". . . all these things happened unto them for examples; and they are written for our admonition." Leaving Egypt is a type of leaving sin. Wandering in the wilderness is a type of the life of a carnal Christian who is controlled by his own selfish will and fleshly desires. He does not deny God, but refuses to enter into God's perfect plan for his life. Study the failures of Israel in the wilderness. I Corinthians 10 points out that their failures have a spiritual significance. If we are not careful, we can fail after their example.

5. Use the following reference guide to help you identify and study other Biblical types. This is only a partial list of the many types used in the Bible.

REFERENCE GUIDE OF TYPES

PERSONS:

Aaron/priests   Jesus as our High Priest
Abraham   God the Father

David	Christ as King
Esau	The sensual, natural man
Isaac	Christ, the obedient son
Jacob	Spiritual man as contrasted with Esau
Jonah	Type of Christ's death, burial, resurrection
Joseph	Jesus
Joshua	Jesus as our leader
Melchizedek	Jesus as priest and king
Moses	Jesus as deliverer and ruler
Rebekah	The church, bride of Christ
Shepherd	Jesus as the Good Shepherd

PLACES:

Desert	Temptation
Wilderness	Life of a carnal Christian
Egypt	Sin
Canaan	Spirit-filled life
Gomorrah/Sodom	Wickedness
Jerusalem	Heaven
Cities of Refuge	Jesus as our protection
Rephidim	Life in the spirit

EVENTS:

Historical Events:

| Red Sea | Leaving the world behind |

General Events:

Baptism	Death, burial, resurrection of Jesus
War	Spiritual conflict
Washing	Cleansing

Natural Events:

Fire	Presence of God in favor or judgment
Flood	Judgment
Rain	Blessing
Snow	Purity
Wind	Might, power

Ceremonial Events:

The offerings of Israel:

-The sin offering: Leviticus 4:1-6. A type of the atonement of Jesus through the shedding of blood.

-The burnt offering: The one who offered it acknowledged that consecration to God is necessary for genuine worship. Consecration must be renewed continually. Leviticus 1:1-4

-The peace offering: Expressed the idea of peace and fellowship with God. Part of the sacrifice was burned on the altar to God, part was given to the priests, and part was for the worshiper to feast upon.

The feasts of Israel:

-The Passover: The lamb was a type of Jesus and the blood a type of His atonement from sin; Exodus 12:3-5; 11-13

-Pentecost: The typical meaning of the feast of Pentecost was fulfilled on the day of Pentecost when the Holy Spirit came to the Disciples in the upper room. See Leviticus 23:15-17 and Acts 4.

-The feast of Tabernacles: This has not yet been fulfilled in type. It pictures the great rejoicing in Heaven when the redeemed of all ages gather around the throne of God. Deuteronomy 16:13-15

MATERIAL THINGS:

The Tabernacle:

God provided the tabernacle as a place where He could meet with His people.

-The outer court: This was a meeting place of the people and priests. The curtains which surrounded it represented exclusion because of sin. But because the walls were of cloth, the exclusion was to be temporary. The door into the Outer Court taught there was access to God, the Brazen Altar represented atonement for sin, and the Brazen Laver reminded of the necessity of purification before service.

-The Holy Place: It represented priestly service. In it was the golden candlestick typifying testimony, the table of shewbread typifying spiritual nourishment and fellowship, and the Golden Altar and Incense typifying worship and intercession.

-The Holy of Holies: This was God's special dwelling place. The veil which separated it from the Holy Place showed that perfect access to God was not yet possible.   The ark containing the law taught the justice of God. The mercy seat taught that a just God can also be merciful because of shed blood. Through the tabernacle God showed what He would do in the future. He would provide a way of perfect communion with mankind through Jesus Christ. God would dwell in the spiritual temple of the church. He would also dwell in the individual believer. This means that the typical application of the lessons from the tabernacle speak of Jesus, His Church, and the believer.

Typical Metals:

Brass	Judgment
Gold	Glory
Silver	Redemption

Typical Colors:

Blue	Heavenly things
Crimson, scarlet, and red	Suffering or sacrifice
White	Purity

Typical Foods:

Bread	Sustaining life
Fruit	Increase or multiplication
Honey	Natural sweetness
Manna	Jesus, the bread of life
Meat	Strong spiritual food
Milk	Spiritual food for young believers
Salt	Incorruptibility, preserved
Wine	Teaching: Fermented wine represents false teaching. Unfermented wine represents true teaching.

Creatures:

Birds	Evil spirits
Oxen	Strength or service
Fish	Men
Goat	Sin or the sinner
Lamb	Jesus, the perfect offering
Lion	Rulership
Serpent	Satan
Sheep	God's people

TYPOLOGICAL BIBLE STUDY

Study of _____ as a type of _____

References	**Event**	**References**

APPENDIX

ADDITIONAL BIBLE STUDY METHODS

The methods of creative Bible study discussed in this course were those which provide the greatest spiritual benefits in terms of application to life and ministry. Several additional Bible study methods are described in this Appendix. While these methods are interesting and will expand your knowledge of the Bible, they are not as applicable to Christian living as those previously explained. For this reason we have provided only a brief description of these methods.

THE POLITICAL METHOD:

The political method studies matters related to the politics of nations in the Bible. It provides understanding of the governments of nations in which Biblical events occurred. To do such a study you must identify:

I.   The type of government: For example, is it a dictatorship or a constitutional government?

II.   Philosophy of government: Is it a democratic philosophy or otherwise?

III.   Geography of government:

      A.   Area governed.
      B.   Organization of subdivisions.
      C.   Seats of government.
      D.   Influence of geography on the government.

IV.   Leaders in government.

V.   Functions of government.

      A.   Administration.
      B.   Public finance.
      C.   War and international relations.
      D.   Judicial affairs.

VI.   Influence of religious groups on government.

VII.   How this government affected the Biblical events which you are studying.

THE PSYCHOLOGICAL METHOD:

The psychological method examines the behavior, traits, feelings, and attitudes of people in the Bible. It attempts to determine the motive or reason behind their behavior. Examples of psychological studies include the following:

1. Examination of the motives for Christian service in Philippians 1:14-19.
2. Study of the influence of Solomon's environment on his political policies.
3. A study of the human emotions experienced by Jesus.
4. An investigation of the Pharisee's actions and reactions towards Jesus.
5. A study of the actions and attitudes of Elijah after the Mt. Carmel incident.
6. A study of the motives behind the opposition to Nehemiah rebuilding the walls of Jerusalem.

THE SCIENTIFIC METHOD:

The scientific method of study deals with scientific subjects in the Bible. For example, you could study the plants, animals, or minerals of the Bible. To do this type of study, identify the subject you are studying and the references where it is mentioned, then determine its spiritual significance. Here is an example of how such a study increases background knowledge of Bible truths:

Subject: Mustard (seed and plant)

Use In Scripture: Matthew 13:31; 17:20; Mark 4:31; Luke 13:19; 17:6

Spiritual Application: The mustard plant sometimes grows to a height of 12 feet. This plant is used by Jesus to illustrate the Kingdom of God and faith. The small beginning of the Kingdom are illustrated by the tiny mustard seed. Although at the start it is insignificant, in the end the mustard seed develops into a large tree. This illustrates the growth of the Kingdom of God. Jesus also said that if men will have faith as big as a grain of mustard seed they can do great things.

SOCIOLOGICAL METHOD:

The sociological method is the study of society. It is the study of groups, group behavior, and relationships within a group. The sociological method includes the study of family, community, government, and social institutions, communication, travel, distribution of goods, labor and management relations, race, religion, education recreation, and the arts. An example of such a study would be a comparison of social relationships in Ephesians 5:21-6:9 and Colossians 3:18-4:1. Another example for study is the role of women in various Biblical societies.

ANTHROPOLOGICAL METHOD:

Anthropology is the study of man, his language, culture, physical development, and history. The history of man is often studied through archaeology which examines the remains of past civilizations. An example of <u>language</u> study would be a comparison of languages at the tower of Babel (Genesis 11) with the gift of tongues on the day of Pentecost (Acts 4). A study of Biblical <u>culture</u> would be studies of the religion, art, music, science, and literature of Bible times. For example, you might study the music of Israel and the instruments mentioned in the Bible.

BIBLE STUDY FILES

It is important to organize your Bible study notes. You may want to study the same topic, book, or passage again at a later time. You will also want to share what you have learned with others.

The easiest way to organize your notes is to create Bible study files. A file is a paper or cardboard folder in which you can place your notes. You can also add articles from newspapers or magazines which relate to the subject as well as notes you take as you listen to others teach on the topic.

You can purchase commercially made file folders at a stationary or business supply store. If you cannot obtain file folders you can make your own. If paper is scarce you can even use old newspaper to create your file folders! To make a file folder use a piece of paper approximately 16 inches by 22 long. Fold it as shown below:

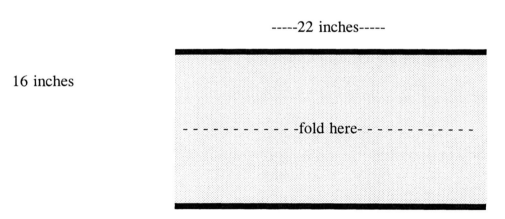

-----22 inches-----

16 inches

- - - - - - - - - - -fold here- - - - - - - - - - -

When your file folder is folded properly, one edge will extend beyond the other:

Title of file

- - - - - - - Top of file with name which reflects its content (Regular file folders have a tab for this purpose)

- - - - - - - Bottom edge folded up

- - - - - - - Place where fold was made

Store your folders in proper order. If you cannot purchase a filing cabinet then obtain wood or cardboard boxes in which to organize your files. There are three main types of files which you should create and organize:

1. Books Of The Bible: Make a folder for each book of the Bible. Place in these folders the notes from your study of that book, its chapters, paragraphs, verses, and words. Organize these folders in your file box in the same order as the books are organized in the Bible, starting with Genesis and ending with Revelation. You will make one folder for each book of the Bible.

2. Topics: As you study various topics, create folders by subject name. For example, you might study prayer, the parables of Jesus, or the names of God. Make a folder for each subject and place your study notes in it. Organize these folders in your file box alphabetically by subject name.

3. Personalities: These files will contain biographical studies. Label them by name, i.e., "Moses," "David," "Joseph," etc. Organize these folders in your file box in alphabetical order by name.

ANSWERS TO SELF-TESTS

<u>**CHAPTER ONE**</u>:

1. All Scripture is given by inspiration of God, and is profitable for doctrine, for reproof, for correction, for instruction in righteousness: That the man of God may be perfect, thoroughly furnished unto all good works. (II Timothy 3:16-17)

2. The word "Bible" means "the books."

3. The word "Scripture" means "sacred writings."

4. Old Testament and New Testament.

5. 66.

6. Law, history, poetry, prophecy.

7. Gospels, history, letters, prophecy.

8. The word "testament" means "covenant."

9. For doctrine, reproof, correction, instruction in righteousness. (II Timothy 3:16-17)

10. The Bible contains no contradictions and it is united in its major theme.

11. The Bible has variety.

12. a. T; b. T; c. F; d. F; e. F

13. Jesus. Luke 24:44-48.

<u>**CHAPTER TWO**</u>:

1. Let my cry come near before thee, O Lord; give me understanding according to thy Word. (Psalm 119:169)

2. 39

3. 27

4. If you just read a chapter here and there you fail to understand how the Bible fits together. You must read the Bible in an orderly way if you are to understand its content.

5.
-Read daily.
-Read selectively.
-Read prayerfully.
-Read systematically.

CHAPTER THREE:

1. The Lord gave the Word: great was the company of those that published it. (Psalm 68:11)

2. A version is a Bible written in a language different from the languages in which God's Word was originally written.

3. A translation is a word by word translation of the Greek, Hebrew, and Aramic words. A paraphrase does not translate word for word. It is translated thought by thought.

4. The King James version.

5. Because no two languages are exactly alike so differences occur when translation is done.

6. Hebrew, Aramic, and Greek.

CHAPTER FOUR:

1. He that is of God heareth God's words: ye therefore hear them not, because ye are not of God. (John 8:47)

2. Because they try to read it the same way they do any other book.

3. Something you must do before you can do something else.

4. Knowing God and accepting Jesus Christ as Savior.

5. Believers who are called as teachers.   The Holy Spirit.

6. The Holy Spirit.

7. The milk is the simple truths of the Word of God.

8. The meat is the deeper spiritual truths of the Bible which are not so easily understood.

9.
-Desire the milk.
-Be obedient to God's Word.
-Search for the meat.

10.
-Set a special time each day to study.
-Select a special place to study.
-Start each study session with prayer.

CHAPTER FIVE:

1. Thou through thy commandments has made me wiser than mine enemies: for they are ever with me. I have more understanding than all my teachers: for thy testimonies are my meditation. I understand more than the ancients, because I keep thy precepts. (Psalm 119:98-100)

2.
-To locate all the Bible references to a word.
-To locate a specific Bible text.
-To find the meaning of a word.

3. 4, 2, 6, 1, 3, 5

CHAPTER SIX:

1. Study to show thyself approved unto God, a workman that needeth not to be ashamed, rightly dividing the word of truth. (II Timothy 2:15)

2. It means you must understand what is being said to whom. You must also interpret and apply the meaning correctly.

3. The verbal inspiration of the Bible means every word in the original manuscripts was inspired by God.

4. The plenary inspiration of the Bible means the full inspiration of all Scripture as opposed to partial inspiration. Every portion of the Bible is inspired.

5. The rules and explanations are as follows:

    1. The rule of divine authority. We accept the Bible as the final authority because it is inspired by God.

2. The rule of literal interpretation. The Bible means exactly what it says.

3. The rule of contextual consideration. Each verse must be studied in relation to its context.

4. The rule of first mention. The first time a word, phrase, object, or incident is mentioned in the Bible, it gives the key to its meaning anywhere else it is used in the Bible.

5. The rule of repetition. When something is repeated in the Bible it deserves special attention as it is very important.

6. The rule of cumulative revelation. The full truth of God's Word on any subject must not be gathered from an isolated passage. The cumulative (total) revelation of all the Bible says regarding a truth must be considered.

CHAPTER SEVEN:

1. Concerning thy testimonies, I have known of old that thou hast founded them for ever. (Psalm 119:152)

2. k, l, c, d, e, g, f, j, h, i, b, a

3. When.

4. Biblical archaeology is the study of remains found in Bible lands. It is a science which gains knowledge of Bible times from the study of existing remains of their civilizations.

CHAPTER EIGHT:

1. The righteousness of thy testimonies is everlasting: give me understanding, and I shall live. (Psalm 119:144)

2. The second main point should not come under point I. It should be a separate point and indicated by the Roman numerals II. Review the instructions for outlining given in this chapter.

3. Horizontally and vertically.

4. Marking is a way to emphasize key Bible passages. You underline selected verses or use symbols in the margins.

CHAPTER NINE:

1. Open thou mine eyes, that I may behold wondrous thing out of thy law. (Psalm 119:18)

2. See the symbols listed in Chapter Nine.

3. See the purposes listed in Chapter Nine.

4. Everyone who claims to speak God's Word is not really doing so. There are false teachers.

5. God will add to them the plagues written in the Word. Revelation 22:18-19

6. Their part will be taken out of God's book of life and out of the holy city and from the things which are written in the Word. Revelation 22:18-19.

7. God.

8. God's words.

9. Milk and the meat.

10. Moses.

CHAPTER TEN:

1. Mine eyes prevent the night watches, that I might meditate in thy Word. (Psalm 119:148)

2. This method emphasizes application of knowledge to life and ministry. It results in increased devotion to God.

3.
-Record passage information   -Identify the subject
-Identify the key verse   -Summarize
-Meditate   -Make application

4. It is not enough just to hear the Word. You must also apply the Word in your life. James 1:22-25

5. Satan fights the use of this method because he is concerned when Bible study results in application which brings positive change in spiritual life.

CHAPTER ELEVEN:

1. Wherewithal shall a young man cleanse his way? by taking heed thereto according to thy word. (Psalm 119:9)

2. 2, 1

3.
-Do an initial survey
-Create a book study chart
-Create an outline

4.
-Title of the book
-Theme
-Author
-To whom the book was written
-Purpose
-Basic life and ministry principle

CHAPTER TWELVE:

1. Thy Word have I hid in mine heart, that I might not sin against thee. (Psalm 119:11)

2. Study of the Bible by chapters.

3.
-Select a chapter title.
-Mark paragraph divisions.
-Create a chapter study chart.
-Create a chapter outline.

CHAPTER THIRTEEN:

1. The entrance of thy words giveth light; it giveth understanding unto the simple. (Psalm 119:130)

2.
-Do a chapter study
-Observe details of the paragraph
-Create a paragraph study chart
-Create a paragraph study outline

3. 3, 2, 4, 1

4. 4, 5, 1, 2, 3

5. 3, 2, 4, 1

CHAPTER FOURTEEN:

1. My tongue shall speak of thy Word: for all thy commandments are righteousness. (Psalm 119:172)

2. Context.

3.
-Study the verse within its context
-Study related verses
-Create a verse study chart
-Create a verse study outline

CHAPTER FIFTEEN:

1. For verily I say unto you, Till heaven and earth pass, one jot or one tittle shall in no wise pass from the law, till all be fulfilled.   (Matthew 5:18)

2.
-Select the word.
-Study the word within its context.
-Determine the meaning.
-Summarize your study.

3. A key word is **one** which is basic to the meaning of the verse. It is an important word. Sometimes it is a **word** difficult to understand or it is repeated for special emphasis.

4. The word "temperance" would be a good subject for word study. The other words are not key words.

5. A concordance and Bible word study book.

CHAPTER SIXTEEN:

1. Therefore I love thy commandments above gold; yea, above fine gold. Therefore I esteem all thy precepts concerning all things to be right; and I hate every false way. (Psalm 119:127-128)

2. The topical method focuses on a selected subject. The goal of the study is to discover all the Bible teaches on the subject.

3.
-Select a topic.
-Select the portion of Scripture.
-Gather the information.
-Summarize the information.

CHAPTER SEVENTEEN :

1. Now all these things happened unto them for examples: and they are written for our admonition . . .(I Corinthians 10:11)

2. The biographical method focuses on the lives of Bible personalities. By studying their lives we learn from their experiences.

3.
-Select the person to be studied.
-Gather the information.
-Analyze The Information.
-Apply What You Have Learned.

CHAPTER EIGHTEEN:

1. 7, 8, 5, 3, 4, 2, 1, 6, 9, 10

2. Thy testimonies are wonderful; therefore doth my soul keep them. (Psalm 119:129)

3. The theological method is the study of basic Bible doctrines about God. The method includes collecting, comparing, and organizing doctrinal statements.

4.
-Select the topic of study.
-Define the doctrine selected.
-Select the Bible portion to be studied.
-Gather information on the doctrine.
-Summarize the information you gather.

5. A "doctrine" is a group of teachings about a certain subject. It contains all the Bible teaches on a selected subject.

CHAPTER NINETEEN:

1. Seven times a day do I praise thee because of thy righteous judgments. (Psalm 119:164)

2. b, c, a

3. c, a, b, d

4. Synonymous.

5. Antithetic.

6. Synthetic.

7. Emblematic.

CHAPTER TWENTY:

1. And He said unto them, These are the words which I spake unto you, while I was yet with you, that all things must be fulfilled which were written in the law of Moses, and in the prophets, and in the Psalms concerning me. (Luke 24:44)

2.
-To authenticate God's message.
-To confirm God's messenger.
-To instruct believers.

3. All Scripture is inspired by God and is profitable for study. Prophecy presents a proper perspective of past, present, and future events in the plan of God. Understanding God's future plan prevents deception by Satan. A special blessing is pronounced on those who study it.

4.
-Recognize Jesus is the basic theme of prophecy.
-Realize that in many cases the Bible interprets itself.
-Understand the rule of double reference.
-Understand prophetic perspective.
-Realize that prophecy is conditional in nature.

5. God.

6. Prophecy means to speak forth under the inspiration of God.

7.
-A message of inspiration from God.
-Prediction of future events in God's plan.
-An interpretation for man of the acts of God.

8. The spoken word and acted prophecy.

9. Genesis 3:15. It is the promise of a Messiah.

10. See the ways of identifying false prophets discussed in Chapter Twenty.

CHAPTER TWENTY-ONE:

1. For the law having a shadow of good things to come, and not the very image of the things, can never with those sacrifices which they offered year by year continually make the comers thereunto perfect. (Hebrews 10:1)

2. The typological method is the study of a person, place, event, or thing as a type of something else. Types give an advance view of what is to come in God's future plan. Although the type is important in itself, it has an even greater significance in the future person or event which it represents.

3. Shadow, figure, pattern.

4.
-Persons
-Places
-Events
-Material things

5. Joseph.

6. Jesus Christ.

Printed in the United States
205847BV00002B/1-36/A